DATE DUE

NOV 1 7 2000		
Dec 8 2000		
Dec 15 2000		
Jan 9, 01		
MAR 15 2002		
Apr 08/08		
Nov 10 08		
NOV 2 6 2012		
NOV 1 3 2014		

#47-0108 Peel Off Pressure Sensitive

LOVE FOR THE LIVING

LOVE FOR THE LIVING

Meditations on
the Meaning of Marriage
and Life

DAN SAFERSTEIN, PH.D.

New York

Copyright © 2000, Dan Saferstein.

Library of Congress Cataloging-in-Publication Data

Saferstein, Dan.
   Love for the living / Dan Saferstein.
      p. cm.
   ISBN 0-7868-6530-X
   1. Marriage. 2. Family. 3. Interpersonal relations. 4. Conduct of
life. 5. Saferstein, Dan. 6. Psychotherapists—Michigan—Ann Arbor—
Biography. 7. Death—Psychological aspects. I. Title

HQ734.S15 2000
155.9'37—dc21

                                                           99-047908

DESIGNED BY JENNIFER ANN DADDIO

FIRST EDITION

10 9 8 7 6 5 4 3 2 1

To my mother and sister

ACKNOWLEDGMENTS

My deepest thanks to:

Herbert Barrows, my dear friend and mentor; you should be given a Purple Heart for all your work in the manuscript trenches; for many years, you were my only reader.

Alan Williams, who died in the spring of 1998; you were always so kind and generous with your time and editorial advice; I used to kid you about being the Bo Schembechler of my writing life; I miss being able to do that.

Angus Wilson, who died in the spring of 1991; you planted the seed that I could someday be a writer and honored me with your friendship long before I became one.

Tony Garrett, who became a friend along with Angus; you never knew how much those postcards I received from you guys meant to me.

Ann Rittenberg, my dear agent and friend; you are the epitome of a warmhearted and devoted professional; I'm convinced that in literary heaven, every writer gets an agent like you.

Leigh Haber, Bob Miller, Martha Levin, Michele Matrisciani, Jodi Glaser-Taub, and everyone else at Hyperion; you've all touched me so much with your enthusiasm and receptivity; I can't tell you how fortunate I feel to have the opportunity to work with such a fine group of people.

CONTENTS

Contents

INTRODUCTION

This book is, in part, about how my life changed when my sister died. Everyone's life seems to change when an immediate family member dies, no matter how close the relationship might have been, no matter how difficult it was to find some common ground. In the case of Rebecca and me, there were times that finding common ground was painfully difficult, and it wasn't unusual for us to go months—once even a year—without speaking to each other. At first, it seemed to be my preference to have a more distant relationship, but as she grew older she seemed to avoid me for the same reason that I had avoided her: we reminded each other of the unhappy family life we once shared. Then something different started to happen in the year before her death. The common wound that drove us apart began to bring us closer together. We called each other on the phone more. We talked about some of the crazy and terrifying things our father did when we were younger. We even promised to share some of our writing, something that we never had a chance to do.

My mother's life probably changed more than anyone's did after Rebecca died, and there was a time when I wondered if she would be able to embrace life again, but she has. You can see in her eyes, particularly when she is around her grandchildren, that she has returned to the living. For the first year, though, much of her was elsewhere; much of her was with Rebecca. It was familiar to me, seeing her in pain, because for much of my childhood she and my father were unhappily married to each other. The main difference the second time around was that I didn't feel alone in my attempt to comfort her. I had children who could sit on her lap and give her pictures they had drawn. I had a wife (or "marriage partner" as Jennifer prefers to be called) who could make her cups of tea and spend an afternoon with her. This meant that I only had to be a piece of the puzzle. This meant that I only had to be her son.

This also meant that I had a family to comfort me. I didn't just have to be the comforter, which is always an uncomforting thing to be when you do it exclusively, when you somehow aren't on the receiving end of all that you're trying to give. It can be a particularly painful experience to try and comfort a parent and yet, if we live long enough and if our parents live long enough, it's something all of us end up having to do. Some of us end up having to do it at a relatively young age—we find ourselves enlisted in the camp of those who have had to grow up quickly—and then it becomes a challenge later on as adults to figure out how to comfort ourselves. It can become even more of a challenge to figure out how to let others comfort us, how to form the kind of relationships where that can happen.

While this book does deal with love and intimacy—including sexual intimacy—it is not about techniques, positions, or the various erogenous zones. It is more a book about the heart, about what happens to the heart when a person feels isolated, as well as what can happen when a person feels a deep connection with a loved one. To a greater or lesser extent, this is a book about me and my families, both the one I grew up in and the one that my wife and I are creating. It is uncanny, as well as frightening, to see how similar these two entities can sometimes be, in spite of how determined we are to make sure that the latter is significantly more loving, secure, and fun than the former. At times it seems almost destined that we must feel pain in the present in order to heal pain from the past.

I will tell you about something strange that happened in the week after Rebecca died: Jennifer and I made love every night. It wasn't something I ever could have predicted, just as my sister getting killed on a motorcycle in Jamaica wasn't something I ever could have predicted, but it caused me to look at sensual love in a different light, a more integrated light, which maybe was in contrast to how I had been looking at it in the years previously, the years Jennifer and I were figuring out how to be both parents and partners, the years I sometimes refer to as my Restless Period.

This isn't to say that Rebecca's death brought our restlessness to an end, or that in the first two years as parents *all* we felt was restlessness, but somehow after she died it seemed easier to appreciate what we had instead of mourning all that we thought we didn't have. This was especially true for me; I was able to let go of some of the resentment I had been feeling as a husband, along with some of the resentment that might have been left over from when I was a son. It often seems to be this way with resentment, that it's left over from something, and even in those cases when it's not, one thing is almost always true: it never does a couple any good. It's not like some of the other feelings that can bring two people closer together.

A few months after Rebecca's death, I came across an advertisement in the sports page that made me think of her and also made me think about writing some kind of book in her memory. The advertisement was for men interested in getting their penises surgically lengthened, something that I didn't know you could do. And the reason I thought of Rebecca was that I knew she would have gotten a kick out of this advertisement if she were alive, that it would have inspired her to write a story about a man who sought a longer penis or a woman who worked in a penis-lengthening clinic. She would have done something funny, something offbeat. The receptionist in the clinic might have worn her hair in a beehive and had a name like Wilma and come home every night to an apartment full of cats. A part of Rebecca was a loner. I think she died without ever having experienced a secure romantic relationship.

And I hope you don't think there is anything irreverent or strange about my writing a book about love and intimacy in memory of my sister, even though this one is more an existential book. I don't think Rebecca would feel this way. My sense is that she'd get a kick out of the idea that there was some sex in it, that it'd be something she'd want to call her friends and tell them about if she were in a position to do so. It's one of the down sides of death, that you can't call anyone and no one can call you, and so I've had to imagine what she'd want included in a book that hoped to embody some of her spirit, a book that might provide an alternate path to the isolation that she and so many others struggle with over the course of a lifetime. I know one thing Rebecca probably would have said: Don't bother having your penis or breasts surgically altered. She'd have encouraged all of us to get our passion enlarged instead. Who knows? As a writing instructor, she might have even encouraged keeping a Small Breast Journal or a Short Penis Journal, since there are some situations where it's more helpful to form a relationship with the feelings we have than to change our outer realities in hopes of these feelings disappearing. I'm pretty sure death is one of those situations. I'm pretty sure love is one, too.

I had a chance to see Rebecca right before she went to Jamaica. She had just finished her first screenplay and came to Ann Arbor full of optimism. She was soaring. She couldn't wait to get to Jamaica to walk on the beaches and listen to the music and eat the tropical fruit. Rebecca had a thing for tropical fruit. Whenever I'd talked with her on the phone, she'd be snacking on a guava, lychee, or star fruit. And before she left Ann Arbor, she pleaded with me to walk across town with her to her favorite juice bar to get guava smoothies. She always had to have a guava smoothie whenever she came to Ann Arbor. So we walked across town with my six-month-old son on my back and got guava smoothies. I had never tasted guava before, and I loved it. More importantly, I loved how good things felt between us. We were having fun. It was a beautiful afternoon. And I remember, as we headed back to my house, I thought of telling Rebecca that I loved her, but for some reason, I didn't. I don't know why I didn't. I suppose I figured it'd make her uncomfortable, or maybe that it'd make me uncomfortable.

It's strange how love can make us uncomfortable.

We then talked for a few minutes in my driveway, hugged good-bye, and she got in my mother's car and drove off. And that was the last time I ever saw my sister.

1

MOURN LOSSES

Together

BEFORE I TELL YOU about the day Rebecca died, or the day I found out that she died, I feel I should mention that my mother is a Holocaust survivor. She is not a survivor of a concentration camp. She is a survivor who escaped Warsaw and spent seven years of her girlhood in fields, Siberian work camps, and orphanages. Actually, when I was growing up I didn't know much about what she was a survivor of. She kept most of her experiences from the war to herself. The one story I do remember her telling me about the Holocaust was when she woke up next to a man who had frozen to death. They were sleeping in a field outside the Russian border in the middle of winter. She was seven then, about the age my daughter is now.

Like my mother, I learned at an early age to keep losses to myself. My losses, though, were much different from hers. They weren't about relatives disappearing or homes being bombed or a way of life being destroyed. They were about subtler and more common things, like tension, like loneliness—not that there was really anything subtle about some of my father's outbursts. I'm sure the neighbors wouldn't have called the police if there had been. And I'm sure my mother wouldn't have filed for divorce after twenty-three years of marriage if their problems had just been subtle.

Unlike death, there aren't many divorce rituals that allow a family to say good-bye to the life they once had. There isn't a funeral and people don't bring over food and visit for seven days afterward. Often people get divorced and nobody even brings over a sandwich. Not that food is necessarily what the divorced person wants or needs. Usually, when a couple goes through a divorce, what they—and their children—need is to be assured that they aren't losers and that the odds of their loving again aren't too bad, that their divorce was more a problem of circumstance than a problem of their inherent lovability.

One of the reasons there aren't many mourning rituals for divorce is that the event isn't as clearly marked as a death. In divorce, nobody is really sure when the badness began and when it will end. Sometimes unhappy family situations just go on and on like a difficult winter, the kind of winter where a snowstorm hits in April, just as everyone is growing attached to spring. Divorce doesn't always mark an end to unhappiness. It can take months, even years, for some people to figure out how to be happy again. Then there are others for whom it can take a lifetime.

Most of us, though, manage to find productive and even creative ways of privately handling losses. We throw ourselves into our work. We exercise. Keep busy. Stay productive. Write. Paint. Sculpt. It's amazing what some people are able to overcome. There is even a fancy psychoanalytic word for this process—sublimation—and it's viewed in a positive light when people do it well. I suppose an example of it not being done well would be using productivity as a means of keeping people at a distance, as a means of preventing future losses; because while we can keep people at a distance, we can't prevent future losses. They come no matter how hard we work. They come no matter how much we exercise.

That all became clear to me one Friday morning on a StairMaster.

In case you're not familiar with the StairMaster, it is an exercise machine that simulates running up stairs, allowing the user to get a cardiovascular workout without having to go anywhere. It can be a convenient machine, particularly on those days when the weather is bad or when you don't have the time or companions to do something else, but I've found that if you use it too much you can get an overall feeling that you're not going anywhere, that you're stuck in some way. Many habitual StairMaster users seem to struggle with some form of stuckness. It can be a stuckness about pushing themselves. A stuckness about hunger. A stuckness about what it means to be attractive.

So I was using the StairMaster one morning—maybe stuck feeling sorry for myself about the temporary rut Jennifer and I were in—when I received a page from my mother. It was the first time she had ever paged me, and I sensed that something was wrong, but I didn't think the wrongness had anything to do with my sister. I thought it maybe had to do with my stepfather, who was wrestling with a number of medical conditions. My sister, who worked for New Line Cinema reading movie scripts, didn't have any medical conditions. She just felt lonely at times. I think her trip to Jamaica had something to do with her loneliness, even though people go to Jamaica for all sorts of reasons. I just knew, though, that one of the harder things to do when you're lonely is to be still, to stay in the same city with the same cafés and people that you've come to associate with your loneliness.

It was like a dream, the way my mother was crying over the phone while people were passing by in spandex outfits and carrying water bottles. It felt like a bad dream that I couldn't stop. Everything seemed to be happening in slow motion. A fitness instructor came up and put her arm around me. I wasn't even aware I was crying. I was aware that my mother was crying, but I didn't have this same awareness about myself. I told my mother I'd get to her house as soon as I could. Then I went out to the parking lot and cried some more, without the fitness instructor by my side, without anyone nearby—but I didn't feel alone. I felt Jennifer was with me, waiting to take my head in her hands, waiting to bring me close to her. It was different from how I used to feel growing up, when it seemed that I had no choice but to fend for myself, just as everyone else seemed to have no choice but to fend for themselves. It was even different from how I had been feeling in recent months with Jennifer, when the demands of parenthood and work and life had left us out of sorts with each other. Ours was a medium-sized rut. We had been in ruts before, but the problem with most ruts in relationships is that you can never remember how you managed to get out of them by the time the next one comes along. It's as if a joint amnesia sets in.

But death will either shake a couple out of their rut or put them deeper in it, and we were fortunate that for us it was the former and not the latter. In addition to being fortunate, maybe we realized that our rut wasn't medium-sized after all, that it was actually much smaller, more manageable; it was small enough that it could be put behind us with just a little effort on both our parts. Not that effort had anything to do with the connection we felt when I drove to her work and told her about Rebecca. Effort seemed more about the little things. The details of living. The compromises. What we felt seemed more about destiny than effort, and I knew right then that as long as we stayed together, as long as we fended together, we would be okay in the long run. We might feel pain along the way, but our pain would bring us closer together instead of pushing us further apart. Deep down, it was something we probably both knew all along, but a combination of stubbornness and blindness prevented us from being able to live out this knowledge, just as so many things prevent other couples from being able to live out the knowledge of their love. The only danger in these ruts, in these periods of dormancy, is that if they go on for long enough the love can go away.

I am a clinical psychologist in private practice, and I remember a client once told me that he believed all love had a shelf life, and at the time I disagreed with him, stating that I thought love had the potential to go on forever, that it didn't have to fade, that it didn't have to go bad; but maybe we both were right in the sense that love has a shelf life as long as it stays on the shelf. Unlike perishable foods, it *gains* life when it's opened, when it's used, when it's savored.

"Someday we'll have to be there for each other when our parents die," Jennifer said, and Rebecca's death still felt more unreal than the eventual deaths of our parents, even though she was the one who was already dead. It was something I had never considered, that the youngest in our family would be the first to leave. I always thought it might be my older brother, Ezra, who had two psychiatric hospitalizations in his early twenties and never managed to put together much of a life after that. But Ezra was here and Rebecca was gone. I would have to go see Ezra and break the news to him gently. How would I do this? What was gentle about your sister getting killed in a motorcycle accident at the age of twenty-eight? The images of the crash and her wounds sent terror through me. What would it do to Ezra? What would it do to my father? I'd have to call my father in Florida and tell him, too—let him know that time had run out on being able to have a closer relationship with his daughter.

Strangely enough, I began feeling hungry and asked Jennifer if she'd walk across the street from her office building with me to get a sandwich. We went to a deli that had been a favorite of Rebecca's when she was a student in Ann Arbor. The woman who took our order looked to be about the same age as Rebecca, or rather the same age that Rebecca had been when she died. It was strange, how she had suddenly become ageless. And I wanted to tell this woman: Don't ever go to Jamaica, don't ever ride on the back of a motorcycle, just stay in the deli where you can be safe; and yet I knew she probably had her dreams just like everyone did. The only difference was that not everyone chased after them with a vengeance as Rebecca had. Not everyone was willing to commit themselves to going after what they loved. Was I? Was the woman in the deli?

I wanted to take her in my arms and have us promise each other that we always would, but she wasn't my sister—I didn't even know her—and so I just took the change from her and put it in my pocket.

2

THINK
As Two

IT CAN BE SO MUCH EASIER to think as one, to think of
yourself, to say "This is what I need," and "This was how
I went about getting it in the past," especially if the past
entailed some aspect of survival, some period of sheer coping, where you had to draw on all your strengths and re-
sources to remain whole, so you wouldn't become a scarred
human being, a human being who, like my brother, Ezra,
can't eat turkey without having to think about what Thanksgiving was like in 1968 or 1973 or some other year when
wounds occurred; and yet Ezra didn't fall apart as I thought
he might when I told him about Rebecca. He didn't take
out photographs from when we were boys—like the one of
us standing in front of our Chevy station wagon. He just
hugged me briefly and said, "Do you know what Mom wants
me to wear to the funeral?"

But most of us, if fate is kind, reach a point where
there is nothing to survive, where the bulk of the adversity
goes away for the time being, and then we must learn to
live, not just by ourselves, but as a team, with a partner

we can trust just as much as ourselves—which goes against everything we learned about survival, especially domestic survival, where the people we love are both the enemy and the ones we hope will save us. Not that it's fair to assume that Ezra's psychiatric condition is the result of a lack of trust, or a lack of anything else, within our family. Psychiatric conditions rear their head within all sorts of family situations, and yet it's probably safe to say that they rear their head more frequently in those situations where there is something to fear.

What is there to fear, though, when you're in your mid-thirties and living out your dream of raising a family with the woman you love? I asked myself this question a lot before Rebecca died. I would find myself in a panic because I couldn't find a bottle of Children's Motrin, or because something else made life feel out of control, and I would say: What is your problem? What terrible thing are you expecting to happen? It wasn't something I could put into words. It was just a feeling I had that if we didn't put our children to bed each night at exactly the right time and give them their vitamins each morning and make everything perfect our lives would somehow fall apart, our family experience would become something that we'd all have to overcome.

Then when Rebecca died it felt that the bad thing had *already* happened and there was no longer any point in standing guard alone, not that there had really been a point in the first place. Guard duty is probably never good for any relationship, especially when it's done alone. It's much better that a couple work out a buddy system for dealing with their fears, a system where they can stand side by side in the face of uncertainty, a system where no one is in charge. Because it's when one person attempts to take charge that things get screwed up the most. It doesn't matter whether that person is trying to take charge of finances, parenting, or lovemaking—teamwork inevitably suffers.

What does this mean, then, if you're in a relationship with someone who isn't acting like a good team player? Should you walk off the court and look for a new team? (Many choose this option, but then they find themselves dealing with similar challenges on their next team.) Some helpful hints can possibly be obtained by watching an NBA play-off game on TV. You will see players yelling at each other for being too selfish. You will see them getting in each other's faces for acting tentative and uninspired. The passion that the players bring to the games is a part of what makes the contests so compelling. Passion makes most anything compelling, just as a lack of passion makes most anything uncompelling.

Here, though, is the difficult part: two passionate people don't always make for a passionate relationship. You have to be passionate about each other. You can't just be passionate about your politics or your work or your art. As the son of two passionate people who ended up divorced, I learned early on that this was true. Then, like so many other people, I had to figure out on my own how to be passionate about love, not just falling in love, but staying in love, doing all the little things that sustain and create love, things like being considerate and empathic and forgiving, things that tend to take a backseat on Valentine's Day to silk underwear and cologne.

This isn't to put down silk underwear or cologne or anything else that can bring about a much-needed sense of playfulness in a relationship; it's more to emphasize that they aren't the bread and butter of teamwork. Any couple who has stayed together over time and weathered the storms that can darken and damage relationships will confirm this. They will talk about friendship instead, about their partner being their best friend. Is your partner your best friend? If not, how have you managed to rob each other of this richness? Because there are times when life will present challenges where you will need more than a lover by your side, times when witty conversation and a beautiful body just won't do. The death of a family member is one of these times. When someone close to you dies, you don't feel like making conversation or being beautiful. You just feel like erupting in sorrow. You feel like being numb with shock. You feel like being with your soulmate, maybe resting your head on her stomach, maybe sitting on a porch swing until the sun goes down. When you have a soulmate, it really doesn't matter what you do with him or her. Everything is secondary to the fact that you're together.

While giving advice might not come naturally for me, I would nevertheless wholeheartedly recommend resting your head on your partner's stomach in those times when the universe feels frightening and unpredictable. It can have a comforting and centering effect, and when your sister dies and the responsibility of planning a funeral falls on your shoulders, centeredness can be a dear ally. The friendship of your partner can be equally dear, because there is nothing stranger than thinking of burying a loved one. And the way some cemeteries do business nowadays— with a Visa sign in the office window—doesn't really help matters. That Visa sign can make it feel as if your loss is someone else's gain. Not that it's the cemetery directors' intention to make you feel this way. They're just around death too much to take notice of the little things. Like the way one cemetery director had her picture on her business card. Why did she do this? What did anyone care how she looked when it came time to choose a cemetery? Incidentally, this was the same director who asked me if I had a particular plot in mind, and when she said this, I felt like telling her, "No, no, I didn't have a particular plot in mind; what I had in mind was a particular life, a life that lasted longer than twenty-eight years." And it felt like my sister and I were heading in this particular direction before she died. It really did. The last time I saw her—about a week before she left for Jamaica—I had the feeling that we were brother and sister. Not prisoners of a common pain. Just a brother and sister who had something to give each other.

But she was no longer around, and so we had to find a different way to continue being brother and sister. I couldn't just call her up and ask if she wanted to be buried underneath a tree or on a hill surrounded by open space. Our relationship would have to move to a whole other plane. A more intuitive plane. A more spiritual plane. What was my part in facilitating this new relationship? I really didn't know. I wondered if it was maybe to just stay open and see what emerged. Stay open. Stay open. I kept repeating that to myself as I stood with Jennifer underneath the tree where Rebecca would eventually be buried.

3

LEARN FROM YOUR
Own Intolerance

SOMETHING all of us should probably consider when we're having problems getting along with other people is this: Maybe it's not their fault. Maybe it's not *just* because of who they are, but also because of who we are—or because of our difficulty accepting who we are. You might have heard the expression that we tend to condemn in others what we condemn in ourselves; well, it's true. It's especially true of the people closest to us. When we love someone, they become our mirror. We see parts of ourselves that we never see when we're alone. Needier parts. Hurting parts. I never used to like the way Rebecca asked so much from my parents. She asked them for money. She asked them for clothes. After my parents were divorced, she even asked my father for a horse, and he bought one for her, but it wasn't beautiful, and the place where it was kept wasn't beautiful, and after a few short months she grew tired of riding her bike to that homely little farm and taking care of that homely creature (it really did look more like a mule) that she maybe initially hoped would take care of her.

It might be easier to feel intolerant of fellow family members than anyone else, because often they are imperfect in the same way that we are. Even those people in our family who are *really* imperfect. Chances are, at the core, they fear the same things. In our family, we all feared poverty. Financial poverty. Emotional poverty. We never seemed to trust that we would get enough of what we wanted and needed. As a result, dinner wasn't as relaxing as it could have been. We all went after the food as if it were about to get up and run away from us. It made for kind of a desperate mealtime atmosphere, which isn't so unusual, from what I've read, for families of Holocaust survivors.

While we're on the subject of food, I should mention that one thing our family had trouble accepting about Rebecca was her weight. She was heavy as a child and suffered in the way that most fat girls do, thinking she should have been something that she wasn't, feeling that she was ineligible for affection, admiration, and touch because she was too big. It was also especially difficult to be a fat person in our family, since our parents viewed overeating as both a personal weakness and a violation of one of their most basic tenets of living: Don't want more than what you absolutely need. In retrospect, we were probably all as ravenous as Rebecca was, but we just chose to deal with our hunger in a more ascetic fashion, almost as if we feared that if we let go of control for one split second we would just eat and eat and eat. This was especially true of my mother, who to this day approaches desserts as if they were as dangerous as cobras.

I can't help but think of a session I had with a couple the other day where the husband felt that their marital problems were due to his wife's weight gain since childbirth; in his eyes she had stopped taking care of herself. He wasn't able to see how the two of them had stopped taking care of their marriage, something that it's all too easy to do once a couple become parents. Fortunately, the woman believed enough in herself to tell him that she thought he was full of shit, but the bad news was that it soon became apparent that was *all* she could tell him, that she couldn't stop herself from going on and on about how he was a coward and a failure both as a husband and as a father, and after a while I had to tell them that I couldn't take being in the same room with them unless they were going to be nicer to each other. It was the first time I had ever said this to a couple. I usually hung in there in hopes that some version of love would eventually emerge, but in this particular instance their hate felt too dangerous, and so I gave in to the need to protect them as well as myself. And sometimes it seems that the couples who express the most hate are the ones who are most afraid of leaving each other and being alone.

Oh, how easy it can be, though, to be intolerant and critical of our partner, of the person we love the most. Some of it has to do with proximity, that our partner's the closest person to blame—aside from ourselves—when we are unhappy. And often it can be more energizing to blame someone else; for the most part, blaming yourself tends to be about as energizing as a high fever. However, it creates all sorts of other problems when you walk around blaming the person you love. First and foremost, your partner won't want to be around you. It doesn't matter how well-formulated your argument is. The gut response is still "Get out of my face." That was Jennifer's gut response when in my Restless Period I would blame her for being tired and inefficient. Then at some point it occurred to me that love was inefficient. The most efficient life is to love no one; in a life like that, you can really get a lot done.

Coincidentally, after Rebecca died, I blamed Jamaica for the same thing that I had blamed Jennifer for: being inefficient. The reason I was so angry at this island country was that days and days went by and they still wouldn't send Rebecca's body back to us. There supposedly were all kinds of red tape because she was a foreign citizen, and because the coroner who needed to process her paperwork wasn't available over the weekend, but in my mind the reason the whole process was taking so long was because everyone involved was getting stoned out of their minds instead of doing their jobs. I couldn't imagine that if your sister was killed in a motorcycle accident in Japan you'd have the same problem. The Japanese would surely find a way to get her body back on the double no matter when the accident occurred.

It's not something you could ever expect to find yourself wishing for: your sister dying in Japan instead of Jamaica.

So we waited and waited for her body to be returned to the United States, failing to realize at the time that when she eventually arrived it would be of no great comfort to us. It was almost as if the reality of her death had somehow slipped our minds, and we awaited the news of her return flight as if it were about to kick off a reunion, as if she would walk off the plane with the other passengers and we would embrace in front of Gate C-9 and say to her, "Oh, Rebecca, you wouldn't believe what a terrible dream we had, how scared and shaken we were, but we're glad it's over, and we're glad you're here with us, and now we just want to put it all behind us and cherish each moment we're together."

But it didn't work like that. We didn't even go to Detroit Metro when her body arrived from Jamaica. There didn't seem to be a point. The funeral home took care of all the necessary paperwork, and then they went to work getting her ready for the funeral. There were just a few details left for me to take care of in the days ahead. Like choosing a casket. Like choosing a rabbi. The choice of rabbi was important to my mother. It probably wouldn't have been important to Rebecca. Any of her writer friends would have been just fine with her. It wouldn't have mattered even if they weren't Jewish. It wouldn't have mattered even if they didn't believe in God. Chances are any rabbi we found would believe in God in a much different way than Rebecca had. He wouldn't think of God in terms of African dance classes or sunny days or great coffee or coincidence.

I didn't grow up in a family where prayer was encouraged.

My brother brought a Bible over to my house a few days before the funeral was to take place, and my first reaction was to think: "Please, Ezra, don't go over the edge right now. Keep a grip on things, okay? Because I can't take seeing you in a halfway house. You have to find a way to be strong. You have to do it for Mom. You have to do it for me." Then I stepped out onto the front porch where he stood with his Bible—the Bible that the synagogue gave him on his bar mitzvah—and I could tell that there wasn't any craziness in his eyes. His eyes were remarkably clear, considering the circumstances.

"I should have been the one who died," he said as he was getting ready to leave. "Not Rebecca."

"Don't say that. No one should have died."

"I would give up my life in a second if it would mean Rebecca could have hers back."

"Why?" I asked, thinking how Rebecca had wanted nothing to do with Ezra before she died, how she was even less tolerant of him than I was, how she saw him as a casualty of everything terrible that had touched our family.

"Because I have less to live for," he explained, and there might have been a time when I would have worried about him going back to his apartment and slitting his wrists; but I didn't, because I sensed what he said wasn't out of self-pity. It seemed to be more out of acceptance, an acceptance that for a moment almost made him feel like an older brother.

4

LISTEN

FEW OF US plan on death teaching us to be better listen-ers. We assume we'll pick up the skills in some other way. Like maybe we'll come across a book that offers some help-ful pointers. There are a number of books out there about communication, even books about how women communi-cate differently from men. What these books can offer, though, is limited if there is chatter in our heads. Chatter about how successful we are or aren't. Chatter about how fair or unfair the world has been to us. Then death comes and brings all the chatter to a halt. It does this by making us feel small, by highlighting how big the universe is com-pared to us; and then once we feel small, our capacity to take more in becomes greater.

I don't come from a family of good listeners. I come from a family of people who had an overwhelming need to be heard, an overwhelming need to be understood and rec-ognized. Maybe you grew up in a similar home, where everyone was trying desperately to get others to see who they were. It can make for kind of a lonely situation. It can make you feel like you're fighting over a pie that's about the size of a quarter. And it's not unusual for a psychologist to be born out of a family like this, the one member to renounce the need for pie altogether and then to reorganize life around providing heftier slices for others.

It's a misconception that all psychologists are good listeners, that they bring to their personal life the patience and interest that are supposedly a hallmark of their profession. I remember a client once told me how lucky my wife must be to be married to such a wonderful listener, and I had to point out to her how sharing a life with someone and sharing a fifty-minute psychotherapy session was comparing apples to oranges. And the truth was that during my Restless Period I wasn't even such a wonderful listener as a therapist. A part of me was often elsewhere. It is one of the defining characteristics of restlessness: the person is never completely where they are.

As for my parents not being good listeners, I will say that it didn't help matters that for much of their marriage they weren't happy together, or more specifically, that my mother wasn't happy. You would think that one person being unhappy in a marriage would inherently make the other person unhappy, but this wasn't always the case with my father. His unhappiness (and happiness) seemed to have a life all its own. He would be up one day for no apparent reason and down the next, and when he was down, it was almost as if he didn't know we existed, which I guess you could say is listening at its worst. And if you are in a relationship where you're made to feel that you don't exist, I would encourage you to protest as vehemently as possible.

You might even have to break your partner's Big Bertha titanium shaft driver, a golf club that runs around three hundred bucks. One woman I knew did this because she felt what she had to gain was far greater than what she had to lose.

In the long run, though, the destruction of expensive sports equipment doesn't make anyone a better listener, especially if that person is depressed or unhappy. Think about the last time you were unhappy. Did you really care about what one of your partner's colleagues said to her in a meeting? Did her grant proposal have any meaning to you? Did you even have an opinion on what she should do with her hair? Because when you're unhappy it seems that the only thing that has meaning is figuring out how to be happy. Until you can get a handle on that, all hairstyles look about the same. So do shoes. Your partner can show you a pair of Kenneth Cole boots and another pair of Hush Puppy loafers and you won't be able to tell the difference. You might not even remember her showing you either pair if you're in a deep enough funk.

But while unhappiness doesn't necessarily help the listening process, grief can make it keener, allowing you to take in *everything*, from a dog barking in the distance to the wind blowing through the trees. There were moments after Rebecca died when I stood so still that I thought I could hear time passing. Of course, I couldn't. It was just something to tell myself, something to distract myself from the horrendous sounds of the day before. My father's wailing was one of these sounds. I called him in Florida and told him that Rebecca had died in an accident and he began wailing like a wounded animal. It actually sounded like someone had shot him with a rifle, and I didn't know what to tell him after that. I sat with the phone in my hand, paralyzed by helplessness. I ended up crying myself, which was what I did each time I had to call a friend of Rebecca's to tell them the news. Each call made it feel like Rebecca was dying all over again, and finally it got to the point where I couldn't do it any longer. I had to assign her friends—the ones who wanted to know if there was something they could do—the responsibility of calling other friends.

Then there were other sounds that were of great comfort to me during this time. Like the sound of our children playing. Like the innocent questions they would ask about the world around them, wanting to know if blind people could drive, wanting to know how candy was made. Even their crying was comforting to me in a strange way, because it meant that they were alive, that they were filled with life, and I suppose my worst fear after Rebecca died was that something could happen to our children, that I could become a heartbroken parent like my mother, as well as my father, who had become the *other* parent after the divorce, the Bad Man, the man Rebecca hadn't had much to do with in the last years of her life.

I couldn't stop myself from going into their bedrooms at night to make sure they were still breathing.

It was also comforting to listen to Jennifer's voice, to hear her wrestling with similar questions about mortality, destiny, and spirituality. Her voice made me feel less alone, and anyone who has mourned a loss alone will tell you that there is nothing more valuable. I will tell you that there is nothing more valuable, and I will also tell you what I came to discover about listening: It doesn't have to be a sacrifice. It can be a way to make you feel better. It can be a precious harvest. This is something that more natural listeners probably already know, but I must go on record and say that I'm not a natural listener. I learned how to listen by listening, and really the best way to learn about listening is to have someone listen to you, which I'm sure wasn't a luxury my mother had either.

Who in an orphanage can really afford to listen?

But I made a point of not withdrawing, of not practicing old habits, of not living my life as if I were in a Polish orphanage—at least when Jennifer and I were together. There were plenty of other opportunities to go inside myself, like the next day when I was at the funeral parlor and the director was taking me on a tour of the casket showroom, starting with the more expensive models, the ones made of mahogany and lined with satin, the ones that cost nearly as much as a Toyota. I knew he was trying to be helpful, but I just couldn't listen to him, because what he wanted to give me wasn't what I needed to receive, and so there could be no meaningful harvest for me in the casket showroom of the funeral home. I had to get outside in the sunshine and listen to my own inner voice telling me that if I got through the next couple of days things would be easier, that the healing would begin after the funeral, after the memorial service, when there was finally nothing left to do.

I chose a simple pine casket because that's what my mother wanted. That's what she told me when we were sitting at the kitchen table the day before. She said, "I want something simple, something simple, okay?"

5

TALK

IT CAN BE EASY to talk, and yet so hard to say what we mean, to put into words what is most meaningful to us in a given moment. Sometimes we just don't know. Sometimes it feels as if nothing has meaning to us. It can be dangerous if we feel this way for too long. I worried that my mother might eventually find herself in such existential danger, that her life might continue to feel fragmented, that she might never feel whole again without Rebecca. It scared me to think of her being fragmented in this way. I had worked with enough fragmented people to know how painful it is to try and reach them. Sometimes you couldn't. Sometimes you just had to form a relationship with the pain of being with someone who was unreachable.

How do we go about trying to figure out what is most meaningful to us in a given moment? One way is to search within ourselves for whatever makes us feel the most. It could be a thought, a memory, or a sensation. It could even be an image—like yellow roses sitting atop a wooden casket. Roses on top of a casket almost always make people feel things. They tend to make people feel even more than what the priest or rabbi has to say about life and what it supposedly means. Not that there was anything *wrong* with what the rabbi said at Rebecca's funeral service. He was a kind man and his kindness came through, but what also came through was the fact that he never knew Rebecca. He was functioning more as a historian. And in the month that followed I would sometimes feel like I was functioning in the same capacity.

As for my mother ending up a fragmented person, deep down I believed that as long as she kept talking about the things that made her feel the most she'd be okay, she'd find a way to survive, just as she had survived the Holocaust, just as she had survived the marriage to my father. Survival was a part of her nature. It was a part of my nature as well, but I wanted to make sure I overcame Rebecca's death in a way that made me softer and not harder. I didn't want to cope as I had coped earlier in my life, by talking about what made me feel the least. It's something we've probably all done before, hoping that whatever we don't want to feel will go away if we ignore it. Inevitably, this strategy backfires, since our emotions don't want to be ignored any more than we do. It is when our emotions are ignored that they seem to cause the most trouble.

However, we all know that it's not possible to bare our souls to every person we meet or to approach each conversation with utmost seriousness. Even if it were possible it wouldn't be appealing for very long, either for us or for anyone within earshot. Within a day, everyone would be yearning for playfulness as if it were a pitcher of iced tea in a desert. Have you ever yearned for playfulness with such intensity? I did when I was in my Restless Period, when it seemed Jennifer and I both had become as serious as a pair of state troopers. You can usually tell when a man has forgotten how to be playful because he will talk at length about his accomplishments or lack of them, which is never much fun for the people around him, and, ultimately, isn't much fun for him either. How can you tell when a woman has forgotten how to be playful? It might be better to ask a woman this, but my sense is that she's often unable to stop getting down on herself. For her appearance. For how her career is going. For what kind of mother she is. For the cleanliness of the house. Often women like this grow quieter with age, for the simple reason that they get tired of telling lies to themselves and the people around them. Then there are those women who discover a newfound honesty and find the whole experience energizing. It is always energizing to be honest. Maybe that's why children have so much energy.

When I refer to people discovering a way to be honest with themselves, I'm by no means implying that this honesty falls in their laps. Honesty never comes all that easily. It is a lot like mountain climbing. Only you are the mountain. The mountain is your fears about being rejected if you present your true self. Are you ready to climb? Are you ready to look in the mirror and say, "I will not live like a waiter any longer, serving up portions of myself that I think people will love." Because once you let go of the fear of rejection the summit is practically yours. You can use your strength for climbing instead of trying to control how people feel about you. It is the first thing any successful climber will tell you: You can't control how people feel about you. They will also tell you that there's really no point in trying, since you don't end up feeling loved even if you get the response you want; instead you just end up feeling that you've managed to dodge rejection one more time.

However, at funerals everyone seems to worry less about rejection. They forget about what their hair looks like and how their clothes fit and where they were educated. These concerns suddenly lose their meaning. They are replaced by the stories about the person who is no longer here. Touching stories. Funny stories. Stories about the things that person loved. One woman stood up and told about the time she went with Rebecca to buy a pair of white go-go boots at a secondhand store, and we all laughed, which isn't something you ever expect to do at a funeral, especially the funeral of your sister who was only twenty-eight when she died; but in the moment that her friend was telling the story about the go-go boots it felt like Rebecca was alive. Her friend's love brought her back for one last minute, so we could all be together, so we could have another chance to say good-bye.

Then we had to take a long drive across town to the cemetery and the feeling of her being with us went away. We tried to rekindle it by playing a Bob Marley cassette of hers, but it was no use. The hearse was behind us, and I kept seeing it in my rearview mirror, no matter how fast I drove or how many turns I took. I longed for her friend to tell another story, but she was quiet. The car's silence was our collective story. I reached across the front seat and touched Jennifer's hand and she smiled at me and I wanted to say to her: "Will you be my sister now? Will you take me to juice bars and introduce me to guava smoothies? Will you share your writing with me? Will you laugh with me about strange things that happened when we were younger? Will you be my family when our parents are gone? Will you be someone familiar at my Thanksgiving table?"

And in my mind I could hear her say, "Yes."

It felt like so much of my life was at the cemetery that day. My parents were there—the second time I had seen them together in twenty years. (The other time was at our wedding.) My brother was there, even though he wouldn't end up staying long. My closest friend, Bennett, was standing behind me in case I needed him. The only people missing were our children, which was by design, because we thought they were too young to deal with the intensity of grief that they would have to witness. And, of course, Rebecca was missing—and would stay missing. That was why we were all gathered: we couldn't keep her from being missing. None of us had the power to change that, and so we had to let go and say good-bye to her. The rabbi had promised that she would live on in our hearts, and while I believed that she would, I had trouble imagining how it would feel to have a sister in my heart and not anywhere else. At the moment the only thing that felt real was the weight of the casket. It was an ugly reality, the way it was lowered into the ground and covered up with dirt. I tried to make it a little prettier by dropping in a blue stone that I had carried with me over the years for good luck, a stone that Jennifer once told me had healing properties. I realized it was kind of late in the game to be giving gifts, but I wanted to give Rebecca one last thing before she was gone. I didn't want her to head wherever she was going without any stuff. I knew Rebecca liked her stuff. I hoped she'd like the rock I gave her.

"Be well, little sis," I said and walked away from the grave and broke down crying beneath a tree.

6

CRY

YOU DON'T HAVE TO wait for someone to die to cry. You can probably find something worth crying about within your own life. Sometimes you don't even have to look that closely. It could be sitting like a pink elephant in your own living room; if you feel disconnected from your partner, that is your pink elephant. You need to start crying about it now, since there is a chance that your tears (and your partner's tears) might be able to loosen the disappointment that has clenched your hearts; and quite frankly, it is a chance worth taking. I say this because the loneliness of a disconnected relationship can feel as terrifying as death, which might be why I have chosen to tell you about what happened to Rebecca and what happened prior to that with Jennifer and me all in the same breath.

Furthermore, if you don't have much crying experience, don't be discouraged, because Jennifer and I didn't have much either. We both went long stretches without crying at all. I think I went about ten years, and within that time my parents were divorced, our house was hit by a tornado,

and my brother was hospitalized in a state mental insti-
tution. Actually, now that I think about it, I did cry once
during that period, and it was when I crashed my parents'
car during my junior year of high school. It was an old
Chevy, but I still thought they'd be pretty upset about the
whole thing, particularly my father. I knew he didn't react
well to property damage—something as small as a broken
plate could render him silent and sullen for days—but to
my surprise, he just looked at the mangled bumper, shook
his head, and said, "You can always replace a bumper."

I have trouble remembering what I did all those years
instead of crying. There are so many things people do instead of crying. My sister ate. She ate so much as a child
that one day my parents decided to put a lock on the refrigerator. It was a bicycle lock with a red cable, and everyone in our family had the combination except Rebecca. It
was an intervention that probably made her feel like crying,
but she would just go eat at friends' houses instead. In the
end, she actually gained weight, which forced my parents
to conclude that they couldn't control her hunger, not even
with a Master bicycle lock.

Can you remember what you did as a child instead of
crying? Are you aware of what you're doing now? A lot of
the couples I see on a professional basis seem to argue,
which is something Jennifer and I did our fair share of
when we were out of sorts with each other. It can be so
easy to argue with someone you love. I suppose this is
because when you love someone it's inevitable that you will
disappoint them and they will disappoint you, and then it's
just a matter of each of you figuring out the best way to

deal with your disappointments, a way that will bring you closer together instead of pushing you further apart. Arguing about who does more around the house tends not to bring about this closeness. Arguing about sex usually doesn't do it either. Most couples find it helpful to take a more confessional path, and what could be more confessional than crying?

But before we can confess an experience, either to ourselves or to another person, we must first believe we have the *right* to feel what we feel. It is much harder to confess a wrong feeling. Wrong feelings tend to get buried and composted into shame. I will tell you a feeling I once had that ended up in the shame compost of my psyche: abandonment. I just couldn't stop blaming myself for feeling alone, which was as unfair as blaming myself for a rainy day. But I assumed that if I were a more cooperative or patient man then I wouldn't feel so abandoned, that I'd be able to bask in a constant sea of cuteness and love like other new parents. Then I began listening more closely to other new parents and it dawned on me that Jennifer and I weren't the only ones who were feeling the effects of trying to provide our kids with many of the childhood experiences that we never had. One client of mine said she sometimes felt like a kamikaze pilot, locked into the cockpit of motherhood, determined to meet the needs of her children at any cost.

Abandonment, though, can be powerful stuff. It can feel like an infection deep within us, an infection that makes it hard to do simple things like clean up the kitchen or take out the trash. Who wants to wash dishes when feeling abandoned? I didn't. I just wanted Jennifer to hold me, and we did hold each other once I stopped blaming her for abandoning me, once I realized that my prior experiences had led me to be an abandonment-prone person. Do you sometimes wonder if you also might be an abandonment-prone person? You can end up this way even if you didn't have a mother who was in the Holocaust. All it takes is getting a larger dose of separateness than you might have been equipped to handle. Nothing more terrible than that. Just separateness. Just the helpless feeling of someone drifting away and there not being much you can do to reel them back in.

When we cry about something in the present it has a way of connecting us to something in the past, and so often we end up crying about the present and the past simultaneously. It is a mechanism that allows old wounds to be healed along with more recent ones; and if you happen to be with someone who is trying to heal an old wound, don't step in and try to take their pain away. Don't even ask them *why* they're crying, because it might get them to stop. It's better to just be with them and not try to figure out anything, which was what we did with my mother the day after the funeral. We sat by her side as she wept and talked, wept and talked. She was holding a box of letters from Rebecca, and it seemed so sad that this was all she had left, a Nike shoe box filled with correspondence. There were letters from Spain, letters from Alaska, and every five minutes or so she would take one out and read it to herself, and it was hard to tell if the letters were making her feel better or worse, because each time she read one it would cause her to start crying again.

We stayed at my mother's house for most of the day, as friends came by to visit and bring food. It seemed that the friends who knew her the best were the ones who said the least, while neighbors and acquaintances felt obligated to talk about the weather or repeat what they had heard about time's ability to heal all wounds. My stepfather, Marv, had gone back to work, feeling a need to have his life return to normal. I didn't blame him for this—it's hard to blame someone for how they react to death—but it did make me think how things would have been different if my parents were still married and they could mourn the loss of Rebecca together, not together as they had once been, but in a more loving and consistent way, a way that could have set a completely different tone for the rest of our family.

Jennifer and I cried in each other's arms when we were by ourselves later that evening. It made me realize how different it was being with someone who was crying when you were crying yourself, when you no longer felt that you had to be the one in control. It definitely felt different from when I was with my mother earlier in the day and she was sitting with her shoe box full of letters. Not that she had ever asked that I be the one to stay in control and comfort her. Not that that was something she'd have ever wanted for her son. It was more a responsibility I had taken upon myself, a responsibility steeped in tradition, a responsibility that had once earned me the esteemed position of being my mother's most thoughtful child, the one who brought her cups of tea and sat with her on the couch when she was feeling down, the one who tried to demand as little as possible, the one who was banking on the notion that if I gave more to her she'd eventually be able to give more to me.

7

Enjoy YOUR PARTNER
When You're Not
HAVING SEX

THIS TIP is probably more for men. It is for men who always need to be taking action, men who have trouble letting closeness come to them. Men like this would make terrible gardeners. They would always want to be digging or pulling up something by the roots. The waiting part would get to them. It'd make them feel anxious, even helpless. And any green thumb will tell you that a big part of gardening is just waiting for the plants to grow.

Does it sound like I'm referring to an unsophisticated man from generations past? I think I'm referring to a lot of today's men, men like me, men whose collective interests keep six or seven sports channels in operation at any one time. It probably wouldn't make sense to an observing alien that a man would choose to watch other men running around on TV instead of running around with his own partner. Who knows what the alien might make of it? She might see how crowded the planet is and assume that these cable sports channels are a part of a population control program.

A part of the problem is that, as males, we are taught from a relatively young age that females are of most value when they're agreeing to have sex with us. It starts in middle school, when their friendship comes to be seen as a consolation prize, as what we get when we are found to be unattractive. We receive the news that a girl *just* wants to be friends as if it were a rejection slip. We feel like we have failed in some way. Our buddies are certain we have failed. They kid us about having to jerk off to a worn centerfold for the rest of our lives. It is our fear that women will never find us attractive and we will feel like the sexually poorest person on the planet. Then we fall in love for the first time and feel like millionaires. We feel special. It is an intoxicating specialness, anchored in the experience that a girl will give *all* of herself to us, that she isn't saving a part of herself for someone who is better. The message is so powerful—and its unfolding is so exciting and beautiful—that we feel good about ourselves in a way that we never had before. We feel victorious, but it is different from the victories we've experienced in sports. It penetrates us much more deeply.

However, as we grow older and get involved in relationships that last longer we discover that the formula for staying in love is much different from the formula for falling in love. Relationships don't last because of our smiles or the definition of our muscles. They usually don't last because of sex either. The reason is that sex doesn't take up that much time. It isn't like house painting. You can have sex frequently and still be left with the challenge of how you're going to spend the rest of your time together.

A relationship with someone you only enjoy having sex with isn't as much fun as it sounds. It might start off as fun, but usually the fun starts waning after a month or two. After a year, someone inevitably feels depressed.

Another advantage of being able to enjoy your partner when you're not having sex is there might come a period in your relationship when you're not interested in having sex. You might lose a job. You might get sick. It is hard to predict what fate will bring. All that you can be sure of is that fate will eventually put you in a dogfight, testing your will, testing your hope. And during the time you are consumed by this fight probably the last thing on your mind will be sex. It is this way with funerals, too. They tend to make people lose interest in sex for a while. The memories of a funeral can be almost as eerie as the funeral itself. The image of the casket being lowered into the ground. The finality of it all. I just couldn't seem to get all of it out of my mind. It gave me chills to think that this was what happened to all of us when we died, that this was what happened to Rebecca, and so I tried to imagine a place that was better for her, a place that was open and peaceful and endless. I would look up at the stars and try to feel the energy of this place, and although it seemed we were so far beneath it, I sometimes *could* feel the energy, could feel a warmth coming over me even if it was a cool night.

Jennifer and I began taking more walks together after Rebecca died. We walked with our children during the day, and sometimes after putting them to sleep in the evening our neighbors would come over and we'd take walks by ourselves. It reminded me of how things were when Jennifer was pregnant with our daughter, Nikki, and we would bundle up in sweaters and jackets and take long walks across town. It was a time when it felt that our lives were still ahead of us, and yet two children later and with Rebecca gone, it no longer felt as if that were the case. We both felt neck-deep in life, and I would have to say that Rebecca's death made me feel suddenly older, closer to the deaths of our parents, closer to middle age and eventually my own death. I began to take more notice of how long people lived. It seemed that you couldn't help but hear of someone your age dying of cancer. It almost didn't matter how old you were. There was a cancer that affected your age group. Lymphomas. Melanomas. It was hard to keep track of them all—and even harder to figure out what you could do to keep you and your family safe.

It occurred to me one day in the park how much more time Jennifer and I had been spending together since Rebecca's death, and I found myself feeling foolish for not having taken advantage of this opportunity sooner. It was an opportunity that had been available; the opportunity for togetherness is almost always available. And in the park I noticed a tree planted in memory of someone named Natasha Bloom. Natasha had only been thirty-four years old when she died, six years older than Rebecca had been. And I couldn't help but wonder about the life Natasha Bloom had lived and what her loved ones had gone through after she died. Did she have any children? Was she married? Had she found something that she loved doing? And I guess I also wondered what it was like for her family when they came to the park and looked at the tree that was planted in her memory. I could see how it would be comforting to see it growing taller each year. Someday the tree would be big enough so that they could sit in its shade. I had no idea how fast a tree like that grew—or if there might even be a chance it could get sick the way a person could. That seemed like too cruel an injustice, for a tree planted in memory of someone to also die a premature death. I preferred to think the world didn't work that way.

8

THINK OF MONEY

As Just Money

THERE ARE so many different ways to think of money. We can think of it as a measure of our self-worth. We can think of it as a measure of someone else's self-worth. Most of us have had the experience of someone in a more expensive car driving by and feeling, at some level, that they are better than we are. Men are probably more prone to feelings of automotive inferiority. Women, in contrast, are affected by homes. They socialize with a couple who have a nicer house and can't help but wonder if they have a nicer life, with less stress, with better-adjusted children.

Have you ever noticed that in the moment we compare ourselves to others we feel less love? We feel less of it if we put ourselves below others; we feel less of it if we put ourselves above others. That is one reason some men have trouble feeling more love—because of this constant comparing. It begins with who can throw a baseball the farthest and ends with who can make the most money; and yet a certain playfulness is lost in the transition to the financial domain, meaning that it is easier to have fun with a boy in love with a game than with a man in love with money. Anyone who has tried playing with such a man knows what I mean. It can be a painful experience, particularly in those moments when the man feels that money has betrayed him.

And I suppose that another way many of us think of money is as a source of security. We assume that when we have more money we'll feel more secure. We even wait to feel secure until more money comes. We do this in our minds. Then we feel strange when our finances improve and we feel just about the same. Same moods. Same level of passion. Sometimes a person's passion will even drop off after becoming more "financially secure," which certainly doesn't make them feel secure at all. It might even make them feel nostalgic for when they had less and were struggling to get ahead.

This isn't to romanticize financial hardship, because it is never much fun to feel poor. I grew up feeling poor, and I used to hate hearing my parents argue about what we could or couldn't afford, my father always being the one to put a halt on *unnecessary* purchases. It got to the point that he once threw a fit because my mother bought a bottle of Heinz catsup—instead of the supermarket brand—and I remember thinking afterward that their marriage probably wasn't going to last long. It turned out I was right, which was less an act of clairvoyance than common sense, given that most marriages probably don't last long when a bottle of catsup can make two people act as if they hate each other.

Whenever Jennifer and I argue about money, I find it helpful to remind myself that we are probably arguing about something else. Here are some things that couples argue about under the guise of finances: control, cooperation, respect, neglect, trust, fear, self-worth, and fun. It is much easier to buy something or to get upset because our partner bought something than it is to talk about a lack of respect or a lack of warmth in the relationship. It is always painful to talk about what a relationship lacks. Sometimes it is so painful that it can take a person months to get up the nerve. Some people never do. They choose either to look for a different relationship that won't lack the same thing or to suffer in silence.

I guess a sound rule of thumb in any relationship is this: Don't tell your partner what they should and shouldn't buy. It is much better to have a common awareness about your financial situation and then to trust each other's judgment. If you can't trust your partner's judgment when it comes to money, that is a different problem. It could be a problem you have in trusting. It could be some other problem that your partner has. Sometimes people buy things to fill a void within themselves. They buy clothes or jewelry or even simple items like Rubbermaid containers. With some people it doesn't matter so much what they buy. They just have a need to acquire and to be out in places where other people are acquiring. In the short run, the whole process makes them feel less lonely.

However, in the long run, it doesn't help to think of money as a cure for loneliness or insecurity or much of anything besides debt. That is one thing money is good for—staying in the black. It makes the math go much smoother at the end of the month when the pile of money is greater than the pile of bills, even though some people don't take the whole equation so personally. They don't see it as a reflection of their character. It's just a math problem with them. It was this way with my sister, who was so unlike the rest of the people in our family, seeking pleasures that were beyond her means, refusing to live in fear of rainy days. It was almost as if she were having a fling with life and didn't care how the chips fell.

And when I went to New York with my mother to clean out Rebecca's apartment I couldn't help but wonder if she was aware at some level that her life would be only flinglike in length. Because twenty-eight years doesn't really give you much time to figure out anything, especially for a writer like Rebecca who might have needed another five years to get back to writing about what was most important to her. It can be so easy for writers to get sidetracked by what they think will sell. I suppose it can be easy for anyone to get sidetracked by a formula for happiness that was either handed down from parents or borrowed from the popular culture. We hear more and more stories about people chucking lucrative careers to spend time with their families or pursue a saner dream, and yet these stories rarely are about twenty-eight-year-olds. The stories about twenty-eight-year-olds tend to be more about moving to new apartments, finishing dissertation chapters, and falling in love—not that there's any guarantee as to when love will make its way into a person's life, or if it will even make its way at all.

But as I sat on the plane with my mother, who still looked numb from loss, I preferred to think that Rebecca was at least on the road to love before she died, that it had become something she wanted more intensely; and because she had wanted it more, the odds of it occurring were much greater. As for my mother, I don't think she was pondering how much further along love's trail Rebecca needed to travel. I think her thoughts were confined more to the reality that Rebecca was gone, that we were about to fly into La Guardia and take a taxi to her apartment and she wouldn't be there. Just her possessions would be there, if that's even what they *still* were; and I say this only because it seems that for something to be a possession there needs to be someone around to do the possessing. A possession can't be possessed by no one. The term implies a dynamic relationship, and yet to speak in terms of *former* possessions made this relationship between Rebecca and her stuff seem too remotely in the past. It didn't do justice to the fact that there was a half-full bottle of juice in the refrigerator waiting to be finished.

Of course, none of this mattered when we were finally in her apartment and faced with the decision of what to do with all the things that she had accumulated over the course of a lifetime. Big things like coffee tables and lamps. Little things like letters and photographs. My mother wanted to box up everything and take it with her, and I tried to be the voice of reason and let her know that just wasn't possible. At some point a friend of Rebecca's came by and took me on a walk of her neighborhood, while my mother spent some time by herself in the apartment. I asked my mother if she wanted to join us, but she didn't. She sat on the floor in Rebecca's bedroom, sorting through her beads, bracelets, earrings, and necklaces. It looked as if she could have spent days there without leaving, and I wished at that moment that someone else could have come to New York with us for the weekend, someone like my stepfather, someone who could have been there for her when I couldn't, when I felt a need to be out in the city, seeing some of the places where Rebecca used to hang out, sitting in the same cafés, eating food from the same delis. I didn't want to stop walking. I wanted to go everywhere she used to go, to her job, to where she took her African dance classes, thinking that maybe if I kept walking long enough I might get a vague sense of what it was like to be her.

My mother was still sitting on the bedroom floor, surrounded by Rebecca's jewelry, when I returned to the apartment. I sat down beside her and asked if I could help with anything, and she suggested it might be best if I started boxing up some of Rebecca's belongings that were less personal, things that her friend said he could take to a local women's shelter. I went to the kitchen, figuring it'd be best to start there, and yet I was surprised how personal a kitchen could be, how frying pans and mugs and a coffeepot could feel so rich in history. There really wasn't anything in her apartment that wasn't personal. Every towel, every plate—even a pair of chopsticks—was a piece of the puzzle that had been her life. Then I came to her answering machine and didn't know what to do. There were two messages that she hadn't heard, that she would never hear. Was I meant to listen to them? Did the people who left the messages know she had died? I pushed the playback button and listened as a friend named Gina welcomed her back from Jamaica, hoped she had a great time, asked that Rebecca call her once she was settled. Another friend, Mira, wanted to meet for sushi, said she had never had it before, but thought it was time she gave it a try, that she finally felt ready to lose her raw fish virginity. Mira sounded a little like Janis Joplin. I popped the message tape out of the machine and put it in my pocket, thinking I'd give it to my mother at some later time.

After finishing up in the kitchen, I went to the living room and found a large jar of pennies on Rebecca's desk. They seemed so lifeless just being in the jar, with no hope of being joined by other pennies, with no hope of being set free out in the world of commerce. I then looked out the window and saw two young Hispanic girls sitting on the steps of their apartment building and took the jar of pennies downstairs and gave it to them. They looked at me in disbelief, as if I were a new breed of Santa Claus, and I wanted to tell them that the pennies were a gift from my sister, but instead I just watched their joyous faces and thought for a second how much better the world would be if people who *had* money saved their pennies, nickels, and dimes in large jars and shared them with those who *didn't*. To my surprise, my mother had a much different sentiment about all this and was upset that I had given Rebecca's pennies away. I tried to explain to her that they weren't Rebecca's pennies anymore, that they were no one's pennies, and I wanted them to become someone's. I wanted to give those pennies life. That was why I had given them away.

9

NURTURE
Friendships

MAYBE IT ISN'T REALISTIC to expect to get everything we need from our partner. Our partner is only one person. The odds of one person being able to share all of our loves isn't good, especially if they're of the opposite sex. Men and women often are interested in different things—or are interested in the same things in different ways. This doesn't mean that they can't love each other, but rather that their relationship needs to be supplemented. If you mind the idea of being supplemented with other people, you shouldn't. It doesn't mean the odds of your being abandoned are greater. It just means that human beings are social animals, accustomed to living in groups. They're less accustomed to living alone in a high-rise apartment with their lover.

For some reason, though, it can be harder to make close friends as we get older. It could be that we are more cautious. It could be that we have less time. Close friendships *do* take time, sometimes more time than can be squeezed in during a lunch or café break. That was what made friendships spring so naturally from youth, that you had whole weekends and whole summers to get to know people. You grew up with them. You lived with them for weeks and months at a stretch. This was long before anyone had a weekly planner, before anyone had daily goals or monthly goals or a five-year vision. Then you just lived. You hung out with your friends when you didn't want to be with your family, when you didn't want to be alone, when relationships didn't work out. You learned that relationships were much harder to predict than friendships. There were fewer reasons for friendships to end. Many of us are still close with the people we hung out with in high school.

But after college, everyone gets spread out around the globe, and they often get busier, and they might even feel they have less of themselves to give, because a marriage can be such a big investment, as can a career; and children can be the biggest investment of all. Children can be the kind of investment that makes you want to talk on the phone less, especially when they're young and you're not sleeping well and you pretty much have to do everything for them. It doesn't matter what kind of long-distance rates MCI is willing to give you. It still can feel like too much work at the end of the evening to put all that you feel into words. And maybe this is how a Restless Period begins: by turning on ESPN and sitting on the couch by yourself instead of picking up the phone and calling a friend. Maybe this is how it begins for men. Women seem to have an easier time sharing the frustrations and imperfections of family life, discussing all the milestones that their children are or aren't reaching, confessing how difficult it is to not have any time to themselves. It is more a man's style to say that "things are okay" and trust that people will assume that within the category of okayness some things are a little more okay than others.

However, when it comes to marriage problems, it isn't always easy for women to confess either. Marriage problems tend to make most of us feel a little abnormal, especially if we happened to grow up in a family that felt on the abnormal side. Also, before you can confess a problem to a friend you have to first confess it to yourself, which isn't something that most of us are eager to do when it comes to our relationships, given the potential for upheaval and change. That is why marriages sometimes have to get *really* bad before a couple is willing to do anything about it; and yet by the time things have gotten that bad, it can be too late for anything to be done about them. When is it too late for anything to be done about your relationship or marriage? When you and your partner no longer like or respect each other.

A tip that could save your relationship: get miserable *sooner* about the problems that you and your partner might be having.

The advantage of talking about a relationship problem with a close friend is that friends can provide a perspective that's neither ours nor our partner's. Or they could provide a perspective that's similar to our partner's, which would indicate that some adjustment probably needs to be made on our part. In other words, it can be invaluable having a close friend who'll tell us when we're acting selfish, since often when our own partner attempts to do this we react defensively. In the worst family situations, there never is this connection with the outside world, and everyone ends up feeling like they're trapped on a sinking ship. What makes the experience feel even more surreal is that everyone leaves the ship each day and returns to it later that evening.

If you don't already have a close friend to confide in, it might not be necessary to go out and meet someone new. You could grow closer with a friend you already have. You could both learn to have fewer secrets and less of a reason to feel embarrassed, because often shame seems to come when you feel you're screwed up in a way that others aren't. When you get to know someone well enough, when you realize this isn't true, the shame starts to go away; it is replaced by a feeling that is so powerful it can transform you. It can make you feel like a different person. Deep friendships have the power to do this.

I had a strange experience when I went to a memorial gathering for Rebecca that weekend we were in New York City. As I was sitting in the YMCA auditorium I felt I was being transformed by *her* friends. Each one stood up and talked about Rebecca and their words changed me. They made me realize how full my sister's life had been, how there were so many people who liked her, not just superficially, but in such a way that it was important for them to fly to New York for the weekend, important for them to tell the others in the room how Rebecca's fearlessness had inspired them to be less afraid, to take the risks they once thought were impossible, like flying on an airplane, like learning to swim, like returning a sweater from Saks without a receipt.

And as I sat and listened to them I couldn't help but wonder how much fuller my life could be if I reached out and touched more people. Because if death came looking for me soon and anyone had cause to hold a memorial gathering for me it wouldn't be very large. There would just be Jennifer and our children and some relatives from her side of the family. There would just be a collection of over-the-hill basketball players. My older brother would attend if his mental state at the time allowed. My parents would be there if they were still alive, but there wouldn't be a crowd of people as there was for Rebecca; and of course Rebecca wouldn't be there.

As the last of Rebecca's friends were walking up to the podium to share their thoughts or stories, I thought of walking up myself, but I didn't know what I'd say, and I guess I also didn't know if I deserved to be up there, if I had been a big enough part of Rebecca's life in recent years to be a part of this loving circle. As I've already mentioned, often months would go by and I wouldn't call her, and while she didn't call me either, I always felt that she had distanced herself because I had distanced myself, that deep down what she really wanted was for us to have a loving relationship, so she could have a family that consisted of two loving relationships, instead of just the one she had with my mother. But that never really happened, or it had only started to happen before she died, and I now didn't feel right getting up in front of her friends and talking about how we *almost* had a loving relationship, or how we *could* have had a loving relationship, because I assumed people at memorial gatherings were less interested in hearing about the possibilities of love and more interested in hearing about love that had actually occurred.

After Rebecca's last friend spoke, I did walk up to the podium, but when I got there I was too choked up to say anything. It took me a couple of minutes to gather myself, to find a group of words that somehow did justice to what I felt and to the person that Rebecca had been. I took a deep breath and finally what I ended up saying was that I never felt as proud of my sister as I did just then when hearing her friends speak so lovingly of her. This was my confession: I was a brother who wasn't always so generous, a brother who would have to take time in the months and years ahead to get to know the woman his sister had become. Then I looked up and could feel the group's acceptance throughout my being, and for a second, I wished that Rebecca's friends could become my friends, even though I knew that would never happen. I never saw any of them after that day. We didn't write or send cards, but I thought of them from time to time, thought of the African drummers who had played music and the people who brought guavas and litchis and the feeling I had for one brief moment, as odd as it was, that something was beginning rather than ending.

10

FIND WORK
That Is Meaningful

I WAS AFRAID to go back to work after Rebecca died, afraid that my clients would be talking about something that was important to them and my thoughts would be elsewhere, like back at the cemetery, like back at our old house where we had lived before our parents' divorce. My mind seemed to have little interest in staying in one place for too long. It would jump from something my daughter had said the night before to something my father had said in 1973, as if time and chronology had suddenly become insignificant. And I couldn't imagine this was a state of mind that would render me all that useful to my clients, even though it was probably easier functioning as a psychologist when you were feeling a bit spacey than at some other job where you were expected to be outgoing and cheerful. How did salespeople do it? How did they go back to work after losing a loved one? What did they do with their grief? Did they make an exception and share it with their customers? Because it is my understanding that this sort of thing is strongly discouraged in the business world, that it is a long-standing premise—or prejudice—that no one wants to buy merchandise from someone who is in pain.

Some jobs, though, can aid in the healing process by putting us back in the current of life for at least eight hours a day, where we can be with people and solve solvable problems and form relationships that even go beyond the job at hand, relationships that can seem to have an element of destiny in them, that can make the lives of everyone feel all that much fuller. These jobs tend to be good for all sorts of healing, not just when a family member dies. Most healing jobs include some aspect of love, even though the term *love* is rarely used in the workplace. It is more common for terms like *team-building* or *customer satisfaction* to be used.

In the field of psychotherapy, the terms *transference* and *countertransference* are used, which to the uninitiated might sound more like terms related to banking or military science. This was how they always sounded to me, and it is probably no coincidence that earlier in my career, when I felt obligated to learn all that I could about these terms, and others like them, I didn't find my work as a psychologist to be all that healing. It was more draining then, more burdensome, and I suppose any job can feel this way when you don't believe that the people you work with have anything to give you.

The problem with having a job that doesn't feel meaningful is that we not only suffer the eight hours while we're at work, we also suffer when we come home—and we cause the people around us to suffer. Children, in particular, suffer when parents hate their jobs. Children see the despair in their parents' eyes and can't comprehend that it has nothing to do with them. Sometimes it can be hard to comprehend this as an adult. Unhappiness is just so contagious. You're almost bound to catch it if you're living with an unhappy person long enough, and once you have it, it can be hard to figure out where it came from—which was probably why I spent as little time with my family as possible when I was growing up. It became a joke with my parents, especially with my father, that I was never there. I remember him once kidding around with a neighbor and saying that I had pretty much left home by the time I was seven years old, that I had taken it upon myself to disprove the old adage that you can choose your friends, but you can't choose your family.

I can recall that when my father came home from work he often looked as if something had been stolen from him, and my mother didn't look all that different. So I pretty much grew up with the assumption that work was something most everyone hated, that a part of being an adult was learning to endure a job that made you feel unappreciated, bored, and controlled. In my father's case, his job as an engineer at Chrysler's tank plant made him feel all of the above things, as well as deeply torn, since while he was designing tanks in his professional life, he was traveling to protests against the Vietnam War in his personal life. If this sounds like a combination that would make a person depressed and numb, in fact it was. My father would sit at the dinner table looking as if he had spent his entire workday staring down a tank's loaded artillery. And while I didn't know until much later, he apparently had felt so down during this time that he had considered taking his own life, something that his younger brother had already done before I was born. I learned all this when I was about fourteen, when he told me that he had come pretty close a few years back to setting himself on fire on the Federal Building steps. He went on to say that the main reason he didn't go ahead with it was because he didn't want his kids to not have a father the way he didn't have a father, and I remember him looking at me as we stood in the driveway as if he wanted me to be proud of him, as if he wanted me to pat him on the back and say, "Thanks for not setting yourself on fire, Dad."

Sometimes, though, we can be dissatisfied with our work when there doesn't seem to be any reason to be, when we're not stuck designing tanks or being mistreated by our bosses, when the problem seems to be more in how we relate to our work than in the work itself. Just as there are people who have trouble embracing any relationship, there are people who have trouble embracing the work they do. For a while, when I was a staff psychologist for a Big Medical Center, I worried that I might be one of these people, since there were days that I dreaded having to put on my badge and my tie and sit in meetings about cost-effective therapy and then having to see patients who were assigned to me because they had a particular HMO insurance owned by that particular medical center. It all felt too impersonal, and I began to feel impersonal, and it is never a good experience to feel impersonal with people.

Then I went into private practice and everything began to feel *too* personal, the way it did in junior high school when it seemed that one missed jump shot or one pimple or one awkward thing you said could jeopardize your whole future, especially your future with a particular girl, who might have seemed so pretty and perfect at the time that it made you feel that you had to be perfect, too. This was how I first felt in private practice, that I had to be perfectly patient, perfectly attentive, perfectly dressed—and that my office had to be perfect, too. I didn't want it to look like the office of a man who was struggling, a man who felt unwanted at times, a man who was downright scared. I even wanted the plants to look perfect, because I assumed that potential clients would think that if I wasn't able to take care of a ficus, I wouldn't be able to take care of them either.

But when Rebecca died it occurred to me how imperfect life was—particularly in terms of relationships—and that it was probably best to view most of them as partnerships in imperfection, which was how I began to view my relationships with my clients. I even stopped wearing a tie. What was the point of wearing a tie if we were both partners in an imperfect world, a world where parents sometimes drank too much booze and brothers died in sledding accidents and sisters got killed while vacationing in Jamaica? I began to feel I had more in common with my clients, even my phobic client, Al, the one whose parents were alcoholics and whose brother was killed in a sledding accident. Al and his brother had been on the sled together when the accident occurred. Al was in back, and his older brother, Tommy, was in front. They were just boys then.

The tree they hit is still standing in their parents' backyard. Al showed it to me one day during one of our sessions, many of which took place in the town where he grew up, the town he was afraid to leave. I could appreciate his need for safety, his need to manage life so closely that further unforeseen losses couldn't occur. And I could also appreciate his need to visit the tree where his brother was killed, because a part of me wanted to go to Jamaica—not that I had any idea what I'd do when I got there. Maybe I thought it'd help me to understand Rebecca better—or to better understand life. At least I trusted this was why Al took me to see the tree in his parents' backyard, so he could understand what died in him when his brother died, and also so maybe someone could tell him that it wasn't his fault, that he didn't need to keep punishing himself, that he had suffered enough already.

As we were standing in his parents' backyard, Al asked me a question that made me appreciate how much my work as a psychologist enriched my life. The question he asked me was if I had any regrets related to my sister, and my first response was that I didn't; but then I thought of a time when Rebecca just started college and dropped by my apartment one evening unannounced and how cold I had been to her, because I was hurrying to get ready for a date with a young woman whose name I can no longer remember.

Then I asked Al if he had any regrets regarding his brother, and he said that he wished he had been the one on front of the sled, which made my regret about Rebecca seem so small, made it seem more like a wave of sadness than a regret, the kind of sadness you sometimes feel when you see someone you care about hurting and it dawns on you that there isn't anything you can do to take away that hurt.

11

LEARN
To Receive

DO YOU FIND that you sometimes resent your partner for not giving you what you feel you need? It could be that you are someone who has trouble *receiving* what you need, which was a problem that I used to have, and probably still have, but now to a lesser extent. Most problems related to loving never go away completely—because of how old they are—but this isn't necessarily bad news. It just means that we need to keep pedaling throughout our relationship, that there is some room for coasting, but that it doesn't make up the bulk of the ride.

And I suppose if it did make up the bulk of our rides then our rides—or relationships—would be less interesting. Can you imagine going on a bike where no effort was required on your part and you didn't feel challenged in the least? I must admit that I always feel more in my element going up a steep hill than going down it, which might also be the case with other children of Holocaust survivors, that they find themselves thriving on adversity, almost needing it in a way.

If having trouble receiving was just a problem that reared its head on birthdays and holidays then it wouldn't be so important, but there are things we need to receive on a regular basis that are much more essential to our well-being than presents. Love is one of these things. We can't expect to feel love if we're not willing to receive it, if we're not willing to slow down enough to let another person's love seep into us. Have you ever tried loving someone who won't stop cleaning or won't stop organizing or won't stop parenting? It can make you want to cry. It can make you feel that your love is as valuable as an apple core, which was how I found myself feeling in my Restless Period when it seemed that the laundry devil had possessed Jennifer's soul. In fairness to her, and to all parents, children *do* generate an unfathomable amount of dirty clothes, but there still were times when it seemed that setting aside an evening to being together would have done us both more good, and in turn our family more good, than having an ample supply of clean socks.

But I grew up in laundry chaos, and so what is tolerable to me probably isn't tolerable to most people. I'm sure the sight of our old laundry room would have sent a chill up Jennifer's spine, and I must admit that seeing it never used to make me feel that great either. It was the most neglected room of the house, with bleach bottles and detergent boxes on the floor, and an assortment of orphaned clothes strewn across a picnic table, and unfortunately it was the room that people saw first when they entered our house from the garage. I remember my friends would laugh at the piles and piles of clothes, and I would laugh with them, but, of course, it wasn't funny to me, and eventually I stopped inviting them over at all. It was easier to spend time at their houses and deal with whatever our laundry room meant to me on my own.

What does laundry have to do with receiving love from the people closest to us? In most cases, probably very little, and yet there was something I felt as a grown man in my Restless Period that was remarkably similar to what I used to feel doing my own laundry as a boy of eleven or twelve. It was a determination, for lack of a better word, to want less from others than they had to give me, and this determination took the form of doing as much for myself as possible, so that I never had to worry about receiving anything from anyone that caused them to feel resentful. I not only did my own laundry by the time I was twelve, but I also bought most of my own clothes (with money I had earned as a dishwasher at a Chinese restaurant) and made many of my own meals. It never felt like I was doing anything out of the ordinary until one morning in seventh grade I spilled hot bacon grease on my hand and had to miss a whole week of basketball practice. I can still remember the look of disbelief and disapproval on my coach's face when he shook his head and said, "Why the hell wasn't your mother making breakfast for you?"

I hate implying that my mother wasn't a nurturing parent. I hate this because of my love for her, and because of her love for me. But it seems that in order to understand ourselves we must become historians of our own lives, recalling to the best of our abilities what really happened, and how we felt about what happened, even if the process reveals the shortcomings and vulnerabilities of the people closest to us. Because it seems that if we're not willing to assume this responsibility of a historian, we end up sacrificing ourselves in order to make the past appear better, in order to protect the people whose love we depended on in order to love ourselves. This isn't to equate the frying of bacon or the washing of clothes with love, since there are countless people whose childhoods were filled with perfectly crisp bacon and neatly folded clothes who find themselves in adulthood with a fear of receiving comfort from their own partner.

Here is an inconclusive list of the fears that people have about receiving comfort:

1. They will become dependent on the comfort and then it will stop.
2. The comfort will somehow make them weaker.
3. The comforting person will make all sorts of demands on them.
4. They will do something to drive the comforting person away.
5. They will lose touch with who they are as a result of the comfort.
6. They will discover that their need for it is insatiable.
7. They will miss out on the opportunity to be in a relationship with a different person who is even more comforting.
8. Depending on it will cause them to lose their drive and ambition.

9. It will remind them of a time when they weren't comforted and leave them feeling sad.

As for my mother, I would like to think that the difficulty she had being a more comforting parent was directly related to the difficulty she had comforting herself and the trouble my parents had taking care of each other. I would like to think this, because it allows me to feel more compassion for her; it allows me to contemplate what kind of parent I'd be if I had been faced with starvation as a child and grew up in orphanages and had to cope with so much death at a young age, which was my mother's story. And if you're a parent who thinks you can comfort your children without comforting yourself or without being comforted by your partner—assuming you even have a partner—then you're in for a rude awakening, an awakening that could launch a Restless Period all your own. It's no coincidence that many couples start having marital problems shortly after they become parents, and it's probably also no coincidence that the two groups of men most likely to have affairs are those who've recently become fathers and those who are approaching retirement age.

Whether you're a man approaching retirement age or a new father or a new mother or a woman of any age, it's not realistic to expect that sex can be the sole source of comfort in any relationship, that you can shun the wisdom, advice, laughter, love, and encouragement of your partner and then expect to make it up in one erotic moment. This might sound like a lecture from an Intro to Love and Relationships course, but you'd be surprised how many people—okay, men—behave as if they need nothing from their partner beyond sexual fulfillment. Maybe you wouldn't be surprised. Maybe you're in a relationship with such a man. Or maybe you *are* such a man. If you subscribe to *Playboy* or *Penthouse*, there's a decent chance you are, since these magazines tend to be targeted toward men who want to receive comfort from women in one way, which tends not to be a way that any real-life women find all that appealing. If you think I'm making this up, just consult a real-life woman. Go up to her and say, "Real-life woman, do you have any interest in forming a relationship with a man who pretends to need nothing from you and then expects that you'll act like a selfless, pleasure-seeking, pleasure-providing robot?"

I guarantee you she'll say, "No."

I feel a bit embarrassed to say this, but I have observed other members of my family associating sexuality with comfort. My research began shortly after my parents were divorced and I visited my father in his sparsely furnished apartment and saw a *Playboy* on the bookshelf and thought to myself, at age seventeen, "Oh, my father likes looking at pictures of naked women, too." It was a revelation that made him seem more like a man and less like a father, and yet much of the divorce process seemed to have this effect on my perception of my parents. My mother had begun dating as well, which isn't to imply that she sought the same things from the men she dated as my father did from his *Playboy*. I remember it being a lonely time for Rebecca, though, because while my father had *Playboy* (and six months later a new wife), and my mother had her dates, and my brother had his Transcendental Meditation and later his mental illness, and I had my sports dreams and the companionship of my girlfriend, it didn't seem that Rebecca really had anything besides a television set and a refrigerator full of mediocre food.

You probably don't need me to tell you that it's never easy to shake childhood loneliness, that loneliness from early in life can follow us around like a duckling, and after Rebecca died I couldn't help thinking that this duckling had followed her to Jamaica, that a part of her reason for going there in the first place was to get away from it, to find someone or something that would fill the emptiness she had been feeling since the days of lying on the couch and watching *Mork and Mindy*. And naturally, I also couldn't help but think that maybe if things had been different in our family and she had come to feel differently about herself and about the potential of being loved in a relationship then she wouldn't have gone by herself to Jamaica and gotten on the back of a motorcycle with a Jamaican man whom she'd only known for a couple of days, a man who died in the same crash she did.

Of course, I didn't share any of these thoughts with my mother, because when a person is grieving—especially a parent—the last thing they need is someone playing Monday-morning quarterback and second-guessing fate. It was bad enough that she was daughterless, that emotionally speaking she was oldest-sonless, that she was essentially left with me, one thirty-six-year-old man, to receive all the sweaters and shirts that she had a need to give, to talk on the phone with when she had a need to hear the voice of someone related to her. I wished there could have been more of me—not for me, but for her—because it was impossible to fill the void that Rebecca had left in her life. Rebecca was so much better at letting herself be mothered. She had a need for it. I once had a need for it. I'm not sure where this need went. To be honest, I don't know exactly where needs like this go, but one thing is certain: they go someplace deep within us. Someplace deeper than restlessness. Someplace that is traumatically awakened when the distance between you and your partner leaves both of you feeling like strangers.

"I have something to give you," my mother said one day when we went to her house for a visit. Jennifer was out with Nikki and Alex in the backyard under a willow tree, the same tree under which she and Rebecca had talked for hours during her last visit.

"What is it?" I asked, hoping it wouldn't be something I couldn't use, something that I'd have to pretend to want in order to not hurt her feelings.

"It's the money I received from the airlines for Rebecca's return flight."

"They gave you money for her return flight?"

"I wrote them a letter and asked them for it," she said, and I wondered what she had written, what words she had chosen to let Northwest Airlines know that her daughter had paid for a round-trip ticket and only lived long enough to use half of it. It wasn't something I ever would have done—caring one way or the other about getting the money—and yet it occurred to me that I really had no idea what it was like to be in my mother's situation. I could only imagine, and as I watched our Nikki and Alex playing in the leaves, even imagining such a loss became too pain-ful to do. I took the envelope of money that my mother gave me and put it in my pocket, and as I was about to walk outside to see if the kids were hungry, I stopped and gave my mother a hug. Actually, we hugged each other. That was more how it felt, that she was hugging me and I was hugging her.

12

FIND A GOOD THERAPIST
When Needed

I WASN'T RAISED to be a therapist or to see a therapist. I was raised to pull myself up by my bootstraps. That was what we did in our family: pull ourselves up by our bootstraps. I remember my father using the expression. It was after my hamster died, and he said that what we needed to do when life knocked us down, when it knocked us down hard, was to pull ourselves up by our bootstraps. I was only seven or eight at the time and wasn't sure what this had to do with losing my hamster. I wasn't even sure what bootstraps were. I just knew that one day my hamster was running around on his exercise wheel and the next morning he was lying dead in his cage.

One time to consider psychotherapy is when all you know how to do is pull yourself up by your bootstraps, because this method of coping tends not to work well in relationships. It works much better in physical tests of endurance like mountain climbing where there are things like ropes and carabiners to rely on instead of people. In a relationship, there isn't much in the way of equipment.

There is just you, another person, and whatever happens to flow between the two of you. The same is essentially true of the psychotherapy, even though some psychotherapists try to wear ties and carry beepers and take notes on a clipboard.

A word of advice: Try to find a therapist who doesn't take notes during your session. You will end up getting a better deal if you can, since more of your therapist will be with you and less will be with the clipboard. It is hard to feel loved by someone who won't let go of their clipboard when they're with you. I guess it is hard to feel loved by someone who won't let go of *anything*.

Does it sound odd that I'm talking about love within the context of psychotherapy? It shouldn't. Love is a major part of psychotherapy and any other healing relationship. You can't be healed by someone—or with someone—who isn't generous enough to share the love in their heart with you. This love can't just stay in their heart waiting to be saved for someone else. It has to be available to you, even though you are a client, even though this love that I'm referring to is different from the love between partners, different from the love between friends.

And, admittedly, it is strange to love someone whom you see in the same office once or twice a week, someone you never eat Chinese food with or watch TV with on the couch, but it is possible for love to occur—or be created— within the rituals of psychotherapy. I say this because it has occurred so many times in my office. I say this because it has occurred with Dr. Bob in his office as well.

But before I tell you more about Dr. Bob, whom I began

working with in my Restless Period and was seeing at the time of Rebecca's death, I just want to say that it is not necessarily the kiss of death to walk into a therapist's office for an initial session and find him with a clipboard in his lap. What *is* the kiss of death, though, is to have a therapist who won't let go of his clipboard or judges you for asking him to do so. Therapy rule #1: Don't ever pay someone to judge you; you can always manage to get someone to do that for free. And while many people—and many therapists—think what's most valuable about psychotherapy is having the opportunity to meet with a trained expert who can point out what's wrong with you, it's always much more valuable to have someone point out what's *right* with you, and have someone point this out over and over.

I'm reminded of what could be one of the most fundamental principles of sports psychology: You can't criticize or punish yourself into becoming a better athlete. It is a strategy that inevitably backfires, to the point that athletes lose interest in participating in their sport. Who wants to participate in something where they will be constantly criticized and punished, either by themselves or another person? I know I didn't when I was in my Restless Period, and yet one problem was that I couldn't quit being a father or a husband or a man the way someone can quit the game of golf. I had no choice but to figure out how to get on friendly terms with myself, so I could then figure out how to get on friendlier terms with Jennifer.

One of the most fundamental principles of family life: When you punish yourself you inevitably end up punishing the people closest to you.

In my case, it wasn't enough that I was punishing myself and the person closest to me; I needed an extra push to pick up the phone and call Dr. Bob, and this extra push took the form of an emotionally starved and frightened client who left me feeling like an emotionally starved therapist. That was her gift to me: she put me in touch with the emotionally starved and frightened part of myself. She did this by wanting to schedule three or four sessions a week. She did this by telling me about the things her relatives stuck into her bodily openings. She did this by asking if I would rub her back.

And if her request creates a picture in your mind of a woman trying to use her seductive powers toward some sexual end, I will tell you right now that is the *wrong* picture. The right picture is of a little girl in a woman's body trying to capture an experience of closeness that she never had, a closeness where she didn't have to be sexual, a closeness where she didn't have to be destroyed. It often amazed me during our sessions that she really *hadn't* been destroyed, that there was so much about her that was likable, that she still had a sense of humor. You wouldn't think that someone who had been sexually abused by two relatives would have a sense of humor. There are people who don't have a sense of humor who haven't been abused by anyone.

However, there was nothing humorous to her about me not wanting to rub her back. We spent the next few sessions discussing how hurtful my rejection had been, and while this might all sound like wacko stuff to you, that a grown woman wouldn't be able to appreciate her therapist not wanting to rub her back, there is nothing wacko about having to tell your therapist when he has hurt you. It might be the most useful thing you do in therapy, especially if your therapist takes you seriously, especially if he's willing to accept that his clumsiness or restlessness or helpfulness can be the cause of your hurt, that your hurt isn't inherently the result of some historical hypersensitivity on your part. A good therapist will apologize when he fucks up. He will know that the psychotherapeutic relationship, like any relationship, inevitably suffers scratches and dents in spite of everyone's best intentions, and that sometimes saying "I'm sorry" can facilitate the repair process more than anything.

How can a therapist's helpfulness be hurtful? It can be hurtful the same way someone giving wrong directions can, like directions that take you twenty or thirty miles out of your way. One of the more satisfying experiences, I've found, is giving good directions when a person's lost. (Pushing someone out of the snow when their car is stuck is another satisfying experience.) The reason, though, it can be so tricky to give good directions in psychotherapy is that often clients aren't sure where they're going, which means it can be hard to tell them how to get there.

I remember for a while in my therapy I would find it hurtful whenever Dr. Bob seemed to try too hard to explain my feelings to me. Apparently, what I felt I needed at the time wasn't explanations, particularly explanations that left me feeling as if I were flunking a class in Jungian psychology. For the record, Bob is a Jungian, even though it tends to be less important whether your therapist is a Thisian or a That-ian and more important he's someone who appreciates you—and he's someone who is making the changes in himself that you hope to make in yourself. There is no point working with a therapist who has closed up shop in his own growth department. That would be as unhelpful as asking a couch potato for exercise tips.

After Rebecca died, my relationship with Bob seemed to change a little, and he didn't offer any of the lengthy explanations—the Jungian monologues, as we had come to call them—that he had in the past. He just listened and asked questions about what it was like to have a family that was now 20 percent smaller than the one I'd once had. And if you're a therapist whose client is wrestling with the death of a loved one, I'd strongly recommend taking an approach similar to the one Dr. Bob took, because the last thing anyone wants or needs when they're grieving is to have death explained or interpreted for them. It is probably better to just keep quiet and learn as much as you can from their experience.

What also seemed to happen after Rebecca died was that I began talking more with Dr. Bob about the life she and I had shared as children. I told him about the time we went out as a family to celebrate Ezra's birthday and how my father refused to order dinner because the restaurant's prices were higher than he would have liked. So he just sat there throughout the meal without saying anything. He sat there looking like a serial killer with a stone-cold look on his face. Even the waiter was scared and went and got the manager, who came to our table to see what was wrong; but my father wouldn't talk to him either. It was as if someone had put a bullet into the part of his brain that controlled talking. Then on the way home he sideswiped a car going fifty and took off without stopping or waiting for the cops, and as the tires squealed and Rebecca began crying and Ezra sat mouthing "hit and run, hit and run, hit and run" as if he'd had a lobotomy, I thought to myself, "This family is really fucked, this family is more fucked than I ever could have imagined." And then I caught a glimpse of my mother in the front seat and could tell she was thinking the same thing—that the problems she and my father were having had suddenly jumped in her mind to a new level. Whether she would do anything about it was a whole different story, but I made a promise to myself then, at age fourteen, that I would do something about it, that I would do everything I could to stand up to my father so that our whole family didn't have to live in fear of him.

"It's too bad everything had to turn to shit on your birthday," I told Ezra as we were getting out of the car, and my father immediately grabbed me by the arm and said I was grounded for a week, but I told him that I'd already promised a girl to go to the Sadie Hawkins dance the next night and that I wasn't going to let her down.

"You go to the dance tomorrow and you just see what happens," he threatened, and the possibility of what *could* happen was on my mind the whole next day. It was on my mind when I talked with my date in the cafeteria, and it was on my mind later that afternoon when I accompanied Rebecca to her psychologist's appointment, because my mother had trouble getting off work on time.

"Dad doesn't have a gun, does he?" she asked, as we sat in the waiting room and I looked down at a history book that I wouldn't bother opening for the entire semester.

"No, he just has himself," I assured her, and by the expression on her face I could tell what I said wasn't all that reassuring, not that I felt I was really in a position to reassure her about much of anything.

I ended up going to the dance that night, as I went on to tell Dr. Bob, and I must have looked as if I had just landed in the jungles of Vietnam, because the girl I was with kept asking me what was wrong, so I told her I was having some problems at home, because I didn't want her to think that what I was feeling had anything to do with her. It's a night that I can still remember vividly. The tension in my arms. The adrenaline. Her lemony perfume. "Stairway to Heaven" playing as we held each other for the last dance. Then it was time to go, time to head back to the world I had come from. Her parents offered me a ride, but I told them that my brother was going to pick me up, because I didn't want them to see where I lived and maybe see my father waiting for me in the driveway like some psycho. I knew he'd be waiting up for me. No one in our family had ever really gone against his word—not even my mother—and I knew he wasn't going to let this one go. He was going to make a statement, and I could only hope that I had grown strong enough to defend myself or that he was going to be in a frame of mind where he wouldn't hurt me too bad.

Twenty-two years later, it felt unreal to tell another person that I felt I had to protect myself from my own father, that I feared his rage could get out of control to the point where he'd try to kill me, but at the time it felt as real as anything; and the fact that our house was dark when I went home made it more real. I didn't bother turning on any lights. I didn't even go to the kitchen to get something to eat. I just tiptoed up to my room, trying to be as quiet as I could, but when I got to the top of the stairs he was waiting for me in the hallway. He stood in his underwear and a T-shirt with his arms folded across his chest. It was too dark to see his face; really the only thing I could see was the shape of his body and whiteness of his T-shirt and underwear. I walked past him, expecting that he would hit me on the back of the head for starters, but he didn't lay a hand on me or say anything. He just stood in the hallway for a while, then eventually went back to his room and closed the door. And I stayed in my room, unable to sleep, unable to believe that if I closed my eyes for a second he wouldn't come back after me.

While that was one of the stranger nights of my youth, the day I told this story to Dr. Bob was also strange, because when I looked up at him afterward I saw he was crying. He was crying and I wasn't—but then eventually I began crying, too. It took a while for it to happen, a while to think about what a shame it was that I had had to invest so much energy in protecting myself and feeling safe, but then the tears came, and I couldn't help but think of Rebecca and how much she had to invest in protecting herself and feeling safe. She probably had to invest even more of herself than I did, because she was still so young when a lot of the crazy things started happening. She was only eight years old when we went out that night as a family to celebrate Ezra's birthday.

13

APOLOGIZE

When Necessary

ONE OF THE REASONS that apologizing can be so difficult is that in order to do it right we need to let ourselves
feel the pain of another person. We can't just apologize the
way tennis players do when they hit the ball in the net
during the warm-up (or when they win a point on a net
cord), saying "sorry . . . sorry . . . sorry" like guilty robots.
Such an apology will never bring us closer with anyone.
And maybe before we can feel the pain of another person
it is first necessary to feel our own pain, which is why
psychotherapists are encouraged to be in therapy themselves at some point in their training or early in their
careers. For a while, before I began working with Bob, I
was reluctant to start therapy because of how expensive it
was, and then it dawned on me that this was as unenligh-
tened as a firefighter not buying smoke alarms for his
home so he can save a few bucks.

However, there are other ways to feel more compassionate besides beginning psychotherapy. You could try sitting in a quiet room by yourself and thinking back to when

you were a child and how good it might have felt if someone had apologized to you—as well as how bad it might
have felt that they hadn't. I remember shortly after Nikki
was born I would have moments, very brief moments, when
I wished my mother could have apologized for not being
happier when we were younger, for not seeming like she
enjoyed being a mother; because I thought if she had apologized it might have healed a part of me that was having
trouble enjoying being a father more, a part that sometimes
yearned for an existential pause button to push so that I
could love our children without having to get up and do
something for them.

But my mother, for all her wonderful and heroic qual-
ities, is not an apologizer, which I assume, in part, is the
result of having survived a harshly unapologetic childhood.
It was something I thought about more in the months after
Rebecca's death: how life rarely apologizes. It destroys your
home, it destroys your country, it carts off your friends
and relatives like cattle to places such as Treblinka and
Auschwitz; and it doesn't even send a card. Then when
you've somehow managed to put this trauma behind you,
life comes and takes your daughter, takes her without
thinking twice, takes her without even leaving a message
on your voice mail.

No, it is true that life rarely apologizes, and this made
me think to myself when we'd visit on weekends and I'd
see my mother so heartbroken: Oh, Mom, you don't have
to apologize to me either. Just forget about the chaos of
our laundry room. Forget about the fact that we ate Mrs.
Paul's fish sticks more than other families did. Even forget

about the fact that you might have been overwhelmed by what we needed from you. It's all water under the bridge. I can find a way to come to peace with all of it. Trust me, I can.

But it was harder for me to come to peace with how devastated my mother still was even months after Rebecca's death. Her depression hadn't lifted, and in some respects it might have gotten worse, because the shock was gone and so many of Rebecca's friends who had been around in the days and weeks after her death were gone, too. They had gone back to their lives, and my mother was left with hers; and hers had a gaping hole in it, a hole that seemed impossible to fill. Our two children could fill it a little, particularly our daughter, Nikki, who seemed to look and act more like Rebecca the older she got; but even she was no substitute. I guess the bottom line is that people aren't substitutable. You lose someone and they stay lost. You can't replace them with a similar one the way you can with so many other things.

"Have you considered seeing a therapist?" I asked my mother, sensing she wouldn't be too receptive to the idea.

"Rebecca's gone. What can a therapist do for me?"

"She might not be able to *do* anything for you—but maybe she could just *be* with you," I said, and I could tell this whole concept of another person—a stranger—being with my mother while she was in pain was hard for her to grasp, hard for her to visualize as being comforting. And I didn't push it. I knew my mother had her own ways of dealing with things, ways she had been practicing her whole life, and I also knew that there was no guarantee that she'd ever be able to form the kind of healing relationship that I had with Dr. Bob.

It was more a wish of mine that she too might be able to have this experience.

"Did you ever see a picture of my father?" she then asked, taking an old photograph out of an envelope and holding it carefully as if it could fall apart at any second.

"How old was he when he died?"

"He was about the same age that you are now," she said, fighting back the tears, and then went on to tell the story of how he had visited her on horseback in a Russian orphanage a week before he died of dysentery, how the last image she had was of him turning around on the horse and waving to say good-bye.

WHILE SOME PEOPLE have trouble apologizing, there are those who have trouble *not* apologizing. They do it even when, deep down, they feel like saying, "Fuck you." Needless to say, it is never a good idea, from an emotional standpoint, to apologize when you really feel like saying, "Fuck you." You just end up feeling like you've betrayed yourself, and once you have self-betrayal in your back pocket it can become almost impossible to love anyone or anything until you get it out. That is why, metaphorically speaking, we sometimes have no choice but to say, "Fuck you" to someone who insults us, even if it happens to be our partner.

I'm reminded of an incident shortly after Rebecca died where my father had to say it literally to a Hasidic Jew who attempted to destroy pamphlets that my father was passing out at a Peace Now rally. The pamphlets advocated a position of compromise regarding the West Bank issue, and the Hasidic Jew who poured Diet Pepsi over my father's pamphlets didn't believe in compromise. He also made the mistake of assuming that because my father was advocating a peaceful resolution with the Palestinians that this meant he was a peaceful person, which he soon discovered wasn't the case. He discovered this when my father hit him squarely in the face with a roundhouse punch that sent blood flowing out of his nose as if it were Diet Pepsi.

And I mention this story not because I think it's so wonderful when seventy-year-old men resort to punching out political extremists, but more because I felt like picking up the phone afterward and calling Rebecca. I knew that she'd have gotten a kick out of hearing about our father's antics, that she might even have felt proud of him. It was something we both yearned for as children: the opportunity to feel proud of our dad—so that we could have some experiences to offset those that made us feel like losers by association.

Fortunately, I married a woman who neither apologized nor punched me in the face when she was feeling angry, and I say "fortunately" because I don't think I would have learned as much about myself if she had had a fear about my being angry with her, as some people do with their partners, as some people do with everyone. Regardless of whether you're a man or a woman, if you have this fear, I strongly urge you to do all that you can to get over it, since you can't really love someone you're afraid of and they can't really love you. The reason they can't love you is that they'll never get to know enough of you to love; and the reason you can't love them is that you'll never feel like their equal.

When you're in a Restless Period, or when you're in any kind of relationship rut, what can be as important as apologizing, if not even more important, is making the effort to change whatever behavior is hurtful to your partner. Apologies start to lose their meaning after a while when they're always for the same thing. They start to feel like lies, and I'm sure this is something that florists know better than anyone, since they have the opportunity to see so many men buying flowers and making promises to wives and girlfriends, the same men coming in and buying the same flowers and making the same promises on miniature cards. It would be something I'd try to put a halt to if I were in the florist business. I'd put a sign up in the window that said: FLOWERS DON'T UNDO THE HURT YOU CAUSE.

I remember shortly after my parents were separated my father brought over flowers for my mother, hoping she might have a change of heart and get back together with him. I happened to be the only one home at the time and tried to convince him to just throw in the towel and get on with his life, but he insisted I take the flowers and put them on the kitchen table, which I did; but they didn't stay there for very long. Within a couple of hours, they were in a trash can with potpie containers and watermelon rind—courtesy of my mother—and when I discovered them I had to think they were the most pathetic flowers I had ever seen, and I promised myself that I'd never become the kind of man who could only appreciate people once they were no longer in his life.

In the months after Rebecca's death, I found that I had trouble relating to my father—or I should say that I had *more* trouble, since relating to him was never something that came easily for me. It always felt unnatural, the way it probably feels for zoologists when they first start interacting with bears and other dangerous animals. And while in my adult years there seemed to be nothing dangerous about my father, I suppose I had never fully forgiven him for the time when he *did* seem dangerous, both to me and to my brother and sister. At times it almost seemed that I was staying angry with him out of loyalty to Rebecca, that I was feeling what she no longer had the opportunity to feel.

I assume that souls don't feel anger.

One of the ways that adults seem to express their anger in the Modern World is by not calling the people they're angry at, and this was how I chose to express my anger toward my father. Months went by and I didn't bother picking up the phone. He would call me during this time, but I never had much to say, even when I thought it would be nice if I *did* have more to say, even in the moments when I seemed to miss having a closer relationship with him. To his credit, though, he was persistent, just as he had been with Rebecca, who gave him no more cause for optimism when she was alive than Columbia gives its football fans. She didn't even return his calls, something that

I always made a point of doing. And I suppose the main difference between my relationship with my father and Rebecca's was that I had come to accept that he would always be a part of my life, while Rebecca was, all the way until her death, still up in the air about this.

Another difference in Rebecca's and my situation was that I had two children, and for reasons that were beyond me, Alex and Nikki adored Grandpa Stan. They loved his endless exuberance, the way he would go from wrestling to playing catch to singing songs without missing a beat. He was like a seventy-year-old camp counselor, and it brought to mind how he could be this way when I was a boy, too; only then it didn't last as long. Something would always happen to bring his good mood to a crashing halt. And then it could be weeks or months before we'd see it again.

I took a walk with my father one afternoon when he was in town for a visit. It happened to be the first time he had been back to Michigan since Rebecca's funeral, and he asked me a question that caught me off guard. He said, "Can you tell me what I've done in my lifetime to hurt you?" It wasn't a question that I ever expected him or my mother to ask, and quite frankly, I didn't know what to say in response. It seemed impossible to put everything I'd gone through into words, but I did tell him about some of the things that were on my mind, like the night he turned Ezra's birthday into a nightmare, and the night he stood waiting for me in the hallway after the Sadie Hawkins dance, and I also told him that what was probably more hurtful than anything was his foreboding silence, how he would walk around for days, even weeks, without saying anything to anyone, and how eerie it was to be in the house with him when he was that way.

While there was more I could have told him, so much more, I kind of sensed that he had had enough, that it was becoming overwhelming for him, and so I stopped. I stopped because his question had been his way of apologizing to me, and because I felt at that moment that even my father, our family's Bad Man, was entitled to my forgiveness.

14

PRACTICE

Being Friendlier

THERE ARE TIMES when we can be friendlier to strangers and co-workers than we can be to our partners. Have you ever noticed this strange phenomenon? Maybe *strange* isn't the right word. Maybe *hurtful* is a better word. Because what can be more hurtful than giving the best part of ourselves to the people who mean the least to us? And it's something most of us have done before, in the name of professionalism, in the name of compliance, and when you're in a Restless Period months can go by before it dawns on you that you've asked your neighbor how his work is going more often than you've asked your wife.

Did you grow up in a family where everyone was friendly to each other? Did they say "good morning"? Did they say "good night"? Did they ask about each other's day? Did they share jokes at the dinner table that caused everyone to have a good chuckle? I remember one of the things about television that was so compelling to me when I was growing up was how friendly some of the TV families could be to each other. This was especially true when I was younger. I would go to sleep wondering what it would be like to be a Brady or a Partridge; then I grew older and began watching mostly cop shows and dismissed the friendliness of these other shows as idiotic fantasy. It always bothered me that Rebecca would watch these family shows with the same childlike fascination that I once did. She would even talk to the characters as she sat on the couch, as if they were real people in her life. Knowing her, I bet she did this even more when she watched the shows alone.

I have a sense nowadays that it's considered sexy in our culture to be unfriendly. You see it all the time in magazines: attractive men and women modeling Italian clothes with the most sullen, guarded expressions. It's rare that you ever see someone who is all smiles, someone who might ask you how your day is going and then suggest that the two of you meet for coffee sometime. Is there something about attractiveness or style or sexuality that I don't understand? Because I always thought that a big part of sexiness was receptiveness, that sex was almost like a loving, erotic conversation between two bodies, and who really wants to have a conversation with someone who isn't going to say anything, with someone who isn't willing to give of themselves?

As a psychologist in a university town like Ann Arbor, I see a number of students in my practice, and one disturbing thing that I keep hearing from these college-age males is the notion that the best way to get a young woman's attention is to treat her poorly, that the moment you start being nice to her is when her interest begins to wane. I, of course, try to tell these boy-men that they're all wrong, that there is a world of sensual passion that is much more powerful than any of the cat-and-mouse games of the dating circuit, but they think that I'm just an old married fart who is out of touch with the cutting-edge sexuality of their generation. They, like all generations, are convinced that they've made groundbreaking strides in the areas of flirtation, seduction, foreplay, and copulation, even though the reality is that they haven't, that they're basically just following in the footsteps of their elders; and when I hear stories about how they strategically ignore the young women they're interested in, I have to believe they're not following those footsteps very well.

For all you doubters, young or old, of this theory of friendly sexuality that I'm proposing, I have an experiment: the next time you want to have a sensual connection with your partner, or a potential partner, think back to when you were a child and longed to have a playmate. Maybe it was summer and you had just moved to a new city. Maybe it was a week when all your friends were out of town. And once you're in touch with the feeling of wanting a playmate more than anything, go up to your partner and say, "Can you come out and play with me?" You don't even have to be wearing Calvin Klein underwear to try this experiment. You can be dressed just the way you are. Either way, you'll probably end up being quite pleased with the results, because there is something about playfulness that is inherently attractive—as well as inherently satisfying—and this includes sexual playfulness.

One thing I discovered when Jennifer and I were out

of sorts with each other was that while playfulness can be a turn-on, guardedness, or unfriendliness, or outright prickness, can be a major turn-off. Not only can it be a turn-off in a particular moment, but it can damage a trust that might take days, even weeks, to heal. That is why relationships never work well when the man—and it's usually the man—only acts friendly when he's interested in lovemaking; and the reason they don't work well is because the woman is constantly feeling the need to recover from the ensuing unfriendliness. The paradox of this kind of recovery is that the stronger the woman is the longer it might take her to recover. Some women grow strong to the point that they find they've lost interest in recovering. It stops seeming worth it to them. They conclude that life would be easier if they just picked up the phone and called a lawyer.

But when you're the child of a parent who is prone to unfriendliness you can't just pick up the phone and call a lawyer. You can't say, "I'm out of here, Dad. Too much trust has been damaged to make it worth staying." That rarely is an option for children. It wasn't an option for Rebecca, and so she was faced with the challenge of keeping my father's unfriendliness from damaging the trust she had with other people. (I guess my brother and I were faced with similar challenges.) This can be the tragedy of early experiences with unfriendliness; you begin to feel that you've been dropped into the heart of an unfriendly world and must take the necessary measures to protect yourself. In Rebecca's case, she seemed to feel the need to protect herself more from men than women, and as I mentioned earlier, she never really had a secure romantic relationship with a man. In fact, she was only involved in insecure relationships with men, and the few she had never lasted more than a couple of months.

One guy even ended up stealing her stereo.

I remember when Rebecca was a girl in middle school and high school she would be the one that boys would call to talk about their interest in the girls that she was friends with, and I always thought that was such a sad position for her to be in, acting as agent to her pretty friends, spending hours and hours on the phone, and yet never having anything to feel excited about when she hung up. Once when I was eighteen I even lost my temper and told her to quit wasting her time talking to boys who weren't interested in her, and then she started crying, and I felt bad afterward and took her for a drive around the lakes where we lived. I could tell that she wished we could have gone for more drives together, that it was a relief for her to get out of the house and not have to scramble to come up with ways to not feel lonely.

"Why is it that boys don't seem to like me?" she asked as we were heading back toward our house. "Is it because I'm fat?"

"No, it's because they're assholes," I told her, thinking that this was about the most comforting thing you could tell a twelve-year-old girl who had experienced mostly rejection from males throughout her life.

However, in most adult relationships rejection and unfriendliness seem to be more interactive and reciprocal— though not necessarily symmetrical—and that one person's assholery, for lack of a better word, is rarely the sole cause of a couple's problems. This doesn't mean that one person can't take a more active role in creating an unfriendly climate in a relationship, and yet over time the Dance of Unfriendliness, or the Dance of Assholery, always involves two people. Two people arguing about who is the *bigger* asshole. Two people arguing about who was the asshole *first*. If you've ever been in such an argument, as most couples have, you know how maddening and pointless it can be—and how it can take forever to get to the task at hand, which is: What can we both do to create a more loving and satisfying relationship?

It is never easy, though, to be the one to initiate friendliness; it is a risk, much more of a risk than reacting to someone else's friendliness. I was reminded of this a few days after my father's visit when Jennifer came down with a toothache, which didn't put her in a very friendly mood, and, in turn, didn't put me in a very friendly mood. In theory, my friendliness shouldn't have had to be dependent on hers, and yet for some reason it was, even though I knew that she had every right to feel miserable because of her tooth pain, which might be one of the most underrated of all pains. Years later I would discover this for myself, but at the time I was more upset about the disruption to our lives. It was something I had come to notice about myself since Rebecca's death: my tolerance for disruption had diminished so much, particularly when it came to losing things. I mean, I once lost my car keys, and by the way I reacted, you'd have thought another member of my family had died.

And I suppose the difference between unfriendliness related to tooth pain and more generic unfriendliness is that with the former you can trust that it will be temporary, that as soon as everything is okay on the dental front then the friendliness will return; and this isn't a comfort that most couples have when they're in a rut or a Restless Period or some kind of period where it's hard to appreciate each other. And maybe one of the more troubling aspects of relationship problems is that you're never sure how long they're going to last, never sure what's a "stage" and what's a trend for the future. Having a solid history with your partner can help some, and yet most of us probably know of relationships, or have been in relationships, that started going downhill—and eventually straight off the nearest cliff—after a number of seemingly good years.

It turned out that Jennifer needed to schedule an appointment with an oral surgeon to have a wisdom tooth removed, but the antibiotics and pain killers that her dentist prescribed in the short run made all the difference, both for her and for me. She could sleep through the night and she didn't walk around the next day feeling as if someone was driving a nail into her jaw. As for me, I no longer had to feel like the Worst Nurse in the Universe and could get back to being her concerned husband, who admittedly needed to figure out a way to be a little more easygoing and flexible when it came to unforeseen life events. Fate would inevitably throw us a few more curveballs in the years ahead—hopefully not too many as difficult as Rebecca's death—and I couldn't react to each one of them as if they were tragic injustices. I had to show our kids that we, as a family, could deal with a wisdom tooth extraction in the same accepting way as we dealt with a thunderstorm; and yet at the time none of us knew that *this* wisdom tooth extraction would momentarily darken the skies over our family even more than the dental community might have predicted.

I took a walk into town with our children the day after Jennifer's dentist appointment and because of how friendly everyone was to my kids, I couldn't help but wonder what it would be like if adults were friendly like this to each other, if they spontaneously waved and asked questions like "So how old are you?" One woman smiled at me in a store, and I noticed she was carrying several books about the Holocaust, and I couldn't help wondering if she had some personal interest in the subject or if perhaps it related to her field of study. I, myself, had never read a book about the Holocaust. In high school, Rebecca and I watched a Holocaust miniseries that was on TV, and I remember she asked my mother to join us, but my mother politely refused. She told Rebecca that it wasn't something that really *interested* her.

I struck up a conversation with the woman holding the Holocaust books, and she explained to me that she worked with the Shoah Foundation, interviewing Holocaust survivors for a video library that was being created for several museums around the world. I asked her if she interviewed only concentration camp survivors, and she said that she interviewed all kinds of survivors, including children who were hidden in attics, including children who, like my mother, had escaped to other countries. And when I told her about my mother's story of having escaped from Warsaw during the Nazi occupation, she offered me her card and I took it from her and held it in my hand, not knowing if my mother would be receptive to being interviewed about her war experiences.

As I stood with Alex on my back and Nikki at my side holding my hand, I kind of hoped that being interviewed would be of interest to my mother, because the few times she'd told me stories about her girlhood it had seemed to bring out her softer side. I recalled that during those times the tension that was often in her face seemed to disappear, that she would come to life as she recalled her big family before the war, the constant stream of relatives and friends who stopped by for dinner and often ended up staying the night, the lively conversations, the abundant food. It was usually before bed when she would describe her girlhood to me, stroking my head or back as she spoke. These stories always struck me as being so hopeful and vibrant. The only story she ever told me about her life during the war was the one involving her family's escape to Russia in the middle of winter, and her memory of waking up next to a man who had frozen to death. Strangely enough, that was my favorite story. There was a period when I was about seven or eight when practically every night I'd ask, "Mom, please tell me the story about the guy who froze to death." She would always tell it to me in the same careful and gentle tone, and I think over time, it became her favorite story as well, not in the sense that telling it made her feel good, but that telling it made her feel the *most*, and in turn, allowed me to feel a closeness with her that we couldn't always share.

"I hope your mother gives me a call," the woman said, handing me a tissue, and I hadn't even noticed that there were tears running down my cheeks.

"I hope she does, too," I replied, and I picked my daughter up and held her, because she said she was starting to feel cold.

15

EMBRACE

The Present

IT SEEMS TO BE something that children do naturally. You rarely hear a child talk about being happier once they're finished with kindergarten or once they're finished with anything. Children accept the challenge of happiness in the here and now. They rejoice when happiness comes easily. They cry when it remains out of reach. A veteran mother (and grandmother) once told me that children, like dogs, basically have two emotions—they're either happy or they're unhappy—and maybe at some level we're all like dogs, even those of us who fancy ourselves to be moody or driven or complicated people.

Can you accept the challenge of happiness in the here and now? It's always a much easier challenge to accept in those moments when we feel we're pretty good at it, and yet life inevitably brings us moments when we feel we're quite bad at it, when being happy feels as daunting as climbing Mount Everest. And in those latter moments it might be helpful to confess, either to ourselves or to others, that we just don't know how to be happier anymore, that we've been going about happiness all wrong, that maybe we've been basing it on the wrong things (like a promotion or tenure or a house), that maybe we've been using someone else's formula for happiness instead of creating our own, which is something that most of us do to a greater or lesser extent: we borrow our parents' formula for happiness and think it will work for us. But then we have to ask: Did it really even work for them? Or did it just kind of work? And if it only kind of worked, could we accept being kind of happy in the way that they were kind of happy, or might there be some other version of happiness that was more a reflection of our own destiny?

As hard as it might be to confess to ourselves that we don't know how to be happy in the here and now, it can be even harder for a couple to confess this to each other, to admit out loud that the formula for happiness that they once had is no longer working. And maybe the truth about all formulas for happiness, particularly when it comes to relationships, is that they only work for a while, that it is only a matter of time before some updating or revision is necessary. That is why new parents sometimes fall out of love with each other: they don't update their relationship's formula for happiness. They make the mistake of thinking that they can keep using the same formula they had before their baby was born, and when it doesn't work, they look ahead to next weekend, or the next vacation, or to when their children are a little older, thinking that's when happiness will return to them; and yet we all know that happiness doesn't always return to a relationship. Sometimes it loses its way, and I have to admit that there were moments during my own Restless Period when I thought maybe Jennifer's and my happiness had lost its way and there wasn't going to be anything we could do to get it to come back home.

But then Rebecca died and it dawned on me that we couldn't wait until next weekend or until our children were older to figure out a better formula for happiness. We had to get down to business right away. We had to fight the urge to distance ourselves from our imperfect lives, because our future lives would be imperfect as well, and we were only fooling ourselves if we thought this wouldn't be the case, that our future would somehow be magically insulated from exhaustion and disappointment and unforeseen hassles like impacted wisdom teeth. But what should this new formula be? What should I do differently or what should Jennifer do differently or what should we do differently together? These questions still swirled through my head even months after Rebecca's death, because I could foresee the potential for slipping back into old habits, spending more time apart, laying the groundwork for what could become another Restless Period or Numb Period or some other Period that wouldn't be good. I liked to think my concerns would disappear as soon as Jennifer's troubled wisdom tooth was out of her mouth and into a plastic bag somewhere, but I knew what we were starting to go through had less to do with dentistry and more to do with this ancient and nagging tendency that we both had to isolate ourselves.

I had a dream about Rebecca a couple of nights before Jennifer's tooth extraction—or I should say I had a dream *with* Rebecca, because that was more how it felt, that we were together in the way we'd been together the night I took for her a drive around the lakes; only in the dream I was kinder and less preoccupied. I wasn't with her because I felt sorry for her; I was with her because I enjoyed being with her. We were walking through the woods, and she asked me what I thought she should do with her life, and I put my arm around her and told her she should just do what she loved. That was my big-brotherly advice. She was only eighteen in my dream, and I remember that's how old she was, because when we were walking in the woods she stopped and drew two nines in the dirt with a stick, looked up at me, and said, "That's my whole life."

The next day I talked with my mother on the phone and told her about my dream with Rebecca, and it seemed comforting to her, that Rebecca had emerged in one of our dreams.

"Maybe I'll have a dream with her," she said, and I almost suggested that she *ask* for a dream with Rebecca, but I didn't want to come off sounding like a guy working at the local New Age bookstore. Instead, I just mentioned how I had run into the woman from the Shoah Foundation the day before, not knowing how she would respond, not knowing if she was even familiar with the Shoah Foundation.

"I thought they only were interested in interviewing concentration camp survivors," she said.

"No, the woman I talked with said they were interested in interviewing all kinds of survivors. She gave me her card and said you could call her whenever you wanted."

"I could have sworn they were only interested in concentration camp survivors," she repeated, and I could tell
that it was nearly impossible for her to grasp the concept
that others could be interested in her earlier experiences,
regardless of whether she had been in a camp.

Then I hung up the phone and this question occurred
to me: How do we embrace our parents in the present once
we become adults? How do we embrace them when we still
have the vague feeling that they didn't fully embrace us
when we were children? How do we let go of this vague
feeling, this vague hurt, and take advantage of the time
that's left? Because you can't wait to take advantage of time
with your parents until they're sick and there's clear in-
dication that time is in short supply. Often by then it's too
late, and if you've ever been to a nursing home, you'll
probably agree that they're not the best places for taking
advantage of time. The air and the long hallways and the
artificially pleasant lobbies (with pianos and fish tanks)
just don't make them much good for that. It's much better
to try and take advantage of time in a park or a living room
(where either you or they live) or even a golf course, which
would have been a nice place to take advantage of time
with my mother, but she didn't play the game. She wasn't
interested in watching the NBA play-offs either. It was hard
for her to appreciate Michael Jordan's place in history, and
yet I assumed this was the case with most sixty-five-year-
old women, not just those who'd survived the Holocaust.
It's probably what made most mothers of my generation
different from fathers—that Michael Jordan meant so little
to them—but this didn't mean that the thought of someday

losing my mother didn't sadden me greatly. It was hard to imagine having a family of origin that consisted only of my father and brother, a family of guys.

Before Rebecca's death, I never really thought much about what it would be like when my mother died.

But losing one person always makes you consider the possibility that you could lose others, that you could lose *anyone*. It was a possibility that I found myself considering as I sat in the waiting room of the oral surgeon's office, even though I was fully aware that people had wisdom teeth extracted all the time, that it wasn't like having open-heart surgery or an organ transplant. I even had four wisdom teeth extracted myself when I was eighteen and couldn't remember anyone making a big deal about it, including the dentist. He didn't require that I have someone drive me home after the procedure the way Jennifer's surgeon did. I ended up driving myself home. I even ended up going to work the next morning. It was a time in our culture, or maybe just a time in my life, when everyone seemed to relate a little differently to pain, both emotional and phys-ical; there was more emphasis then on biting the bullet, and no one seemed to want to go out of the way to prevent more pain, either by wearing a bicycle helmet or a seat belt or finding a "designated driver" when they were completely wasted.

The oral surgeon said that Jennifer's swelling would start to go down in a couple of days and that her pain would subside, but just the opposite happened; her swelling got worse, because of an infection, and spread from her ear down to her neck. The surgeon prescribed antibiotics over the phone and scheduled an appointment for the following morning, but later that night Jennifer woke up and was in so much pain and was having so much trouble swallowing that the surgeon recommended that she go by ambulance immediately to the hospital. And if you want to know what it's like to be left at home at three in the morning with your two children while your wife is taken by ambulance to the hospital a few months after your sister died, I'll tell you: It feels like a nightmare. The kind of nightmare that puts you into shock, makes you feel numb with terror, and then even starts to piss you off in a way, piss you off to the point that you find yourself talking to the darkness, saying, "God, you took my sister. Don't you dare take my wife."

"Where's Mommy?" Nikki asked, coming downstairs sleepy-eyed in her Lion King pajamas.

"Mommy had to go to the hospital—because of her tooth, but she's going to be okay. She'll probably be back tomorrow."

"Is Mommy going to die, Daddy?"

"No, honey, she's not going to die. She's going to be fine. Now, let me take you back to bed and we'll talk more about it in the morning."

"Blue died from eating too many bagels," she recalled, and our neighbor's dog, Blue, did indeed die from eating too many bagels. This happened at an Ultimate Frisbee tournament.

"That's right. He ate the whole bag. You have a good memory."

"How did Aunt Becca die?" she then asked, and I really

didn't want to be having this conversation with her at three in the morning. I feared it would give her nightmares.

"She died in an accident, a motorcycle accident."

"Was she wearing a helmet?"

"No, I don't think she was."

"I always wear a helmet when I ride my bike, right, Daddy?"

"Right, sweetheart," I said, picking her up and taking her upstairs, since I was starting to get the feeling that she'd be content to continue our conversation for another hour or two.

"Daddy, can I sleep in you and Mommy's bed tonight?"

"Is that what you want?"

She nodded, and I took her to our bed and tucked her under the covers, seeing no reason not to do whatever was going to help her feel safest, and within minutes she was asleep.

16

TRY

Having Children

BEFORE I TELL YOU about the urge I had to reproduce
the day after Jennifer returned home from the hospital, I
should probably go on record and say that children usually
aren't good for a couple's sex life. Young children, in particular, tend to be bad for this, in the same way that caring
for five or six thousand goldfish probably would be. My
sense is that caring for that many goldfish would be about
the same amount of work as caring for one infant, assuming that each fish had its own bowl and they weren't just
lumped together in one giant aquarium. One giant aquarium of fish, no matter how many fish were in there,
wouldn't compare to the demands of an infant and toddler.
And it is these demands that can short-circuit sexual passion—maybe more so in women than men—faster than
watching a low-budget violent movie; because by the end
of the day you can feel like a maid, janitor, taxi driver,
camp counselor, philosopher, nurse, short-order cook,
teacher, security guard, Chinese launderer, and jellyfish all
in one.

I threw jellyfish in there because I assume that jellyfish don't have a strong sense of self, that it can be hard for them to separate themselves from the water they're in, and this is exactly how parenthood can feel at times. You can have days when it's hard to know where you end and the universe of diapers, applesauce, Barney, chicken nuggets, Raffi, Berenstain Bears, ear infections, Motrin, and Pocahontas begins. And most of us have discovered, either through insight or trial and error, that you need to have a sense of self for sex to be enjoyable; that if you don't, it can feel no more enjoyable than a crowded elevator ride.

But that doesn't mean that if you're neck-deep into parenthood and the thought of having sex with your partner doesn't interest you your situation is necessarily hopeless. Any situation where two people love each other is never hopeless. It just might be that your situation is in need of a major dose of creativity, and when I mention *creativity* I'm not referring to anything silky from a Victoria's Secret catalog or an advanced sexual position requiring tremendous flexibility. I'm referring to something as simple as finding a regular baby-sitter for Saturday night, something as simple as taking thirty minutes at the end of the day to be together without children around.

I should probably also add that just because children might throw a wet blanket over sexual passion for a little while this doesn't mean that we shouldn't have them. We pursue a lot of things in our lives that aren't necessarily good for sex. Work is probably one of them. Think how much better sex we'd have if we didn't have to work stressful jobs involving deadlines, meaningless paperwork, a few unpleasant colleagues, and possibly insufficient pay. The truth is we don't make all of our life's decisions based on how it will affect our sex lives. Who knows? Maybe we'd be happier if we did. Maybe we'd weigh the countless choices we made in our week more carefully. Like I could see a man being asked to fly out to Myrtle Beach for a weekend of free golf and him saying, "I'm afraid not, Fred. It wouldn't be sensually advantageous." The same line of thinking could occur in a den on football Sunday. It could be the fourth quarter of a tied game between the Packers and the 49ers, and a man could get up from his La-Z-Boy, turn off the TV, shake his head, and say, "Not sexually a good idea right now."

But I think there is a difference between sacrificing sexual passion in the short run for children and sacrificing it for golf or watching football; because children have the potential to nurture your soul in a way that golf really can't. That is why people take so many pictures of their children—so they can have something to document their souls being nurtured at each stage along the way. It is really less common for people to take pictures of their golf equipment or their TV set, even though that has probably happened on occasion by men who don't know how to let their souls be touched by the people closest to them. I will tell you one of the best ways to let your soul be touched by your own children: Be with them. Not for just a brief session of quality time before bedtime. Not for just the latter innings of a Little League game on a Tuesday evening. But for a big, juicy slab of time—like an entire day or weekend.

I will tell you a story of when my soul felt touched by

our children, something that took place a couple of days after Jennifer returned home from the hospital. It was a Sunday afternoon, and I went with them to the University of Michigan Museum of Art, so Jennifer could have a couple of hours to rest. She was still tired and looked pale, but not as pale as she looked the night she went by ambulance to the hospital. It scared me to think of that night, because not only was she so pale, but the surgeon later informed us that her infection could have been fatal if her infection had gotten any worse, and I just didn't know how to get that word *fatal* out of my mind. It was there with other words like *casket* and *loss* and *heartbroken* and *motherless*.

The fact that Nikki and Alex were so excited about being at the museum was a welcome distraction. It was the first time they had ever been to an art museum of any kind, and Nikki, who was about to turn four, became very excited at the sight of the big colorful paintings. For some reason, the way she enjoyed looking at them the most was to lie on her back and look up at them, the way you might lie on your back and look up at the stars. The big Mark Rothko painting was her favorite. And then after we saw the entire exhibit and went outside, she lay down on the sidewalk, looked up at the sky, and said, "You know, Daddy, the best art project of all is really the whole world."

A final thought on this business of letting your soul be touched: it could improve your sexual relationship with your partner if you become more receptive to it. No one really wants to be in a relationship where they're being deeply affected by you and you're not being deeply affected by them. Such a one-sided relationship can make you feel less like a person and more like an echo, and it is never a good feeling to be in a relationship where you're made to feel like anything but a person. I suppose the exception might be if you're in a relationship where you're made to feel like a goddess, which was how I remembered relating to Jennifer in the latter stages of her pregnancy, when she seemed to get rounder and more beautiful each week.

Maybe I should also mention that not all parents end up sacrificing sexual passion, not even in the short run. Those who sacrifice passion more often tend to be parents toward the emotionally indulgent end of the spectrum, parents who are as determined as ants to make sure that their children don't get even the slightest whiff of abandonment or neglect, parents who for all practical purposes are like Jennifer and me. But there are other parents who manage to keep going out to dinner and seeing all the latest movies without missing a beat, and it's not as if their children seem to show any outward signs of damage. One woman we know went on a week's vacation with her husband a couple months after giving birth and left her baby with her mother, which isn't something Jennifer and I could ever do, even if our parents made such an offer. We'd both be too worried about what thoughts could possibly be going through our child's head when day after day would go by and there was still no sign of our return.

WHILE JENNIFER'S BRUSH WITH DEATH evoked a re-productive reaction in me, it didn't have the same immediate effect on her. She continued to feel tired and just needed some time to get her strength back, so our children, and any future child, could have a strong mom. And yet just knowing that she was receptive, and even excited in a fatigued way, about having a third child was all I needed to feel the rush of reproductive adrenaline and begin the process of imagining what our next child would be like and what she would love and even if she would be a he or she; and this seemed to lead to the process of courting our future child's soul, assuring her that we would love her as much as we loved anything, promising to always have plenty of breast milk on tap, and reminding her that we would do everything within our power to make sure she had the opportunity to become who she was meant to become.

It is a much different experience to court the soul of your future child after the soul of your sister has gone off to someplace else—assuming you even believe all this business about souls and the courting of them—because you can't help but wonder if maybe her soul and your future child's soul might cross paths, wherever it is that souls do this sort of thing, and that maybe they might have some kind of conversation, in a soul-like way of course, going over some of the pros and cons of being in a human body, covering everything from sunrises to milk shakes to rigid teachers to ankle sprains. I could picture Rebecca's soul having a lot to say about life, being a soul's soul, so to speak, because she had so much to say about it when she was a person.

Sometimes, though, I had trouble remembering what her voice sounded like.

I knew it would be a little while before we actually began trying to have another child, so I just tried to enjoy the two children we had, which, together, were plenty of children to enjoy. It was hard to imagine how much fuller life could feel with three, since it felt pretty darn full with two, and yet I found myself drawn to limits of family fullness in the same way that marathoners and mountain climbers are probably drawn to the limits of their physical endurance. It had always been this way with me, that I wanted to someday have a big family, and yet Rebecca's death seemed to intensify the need to have more people on this earth related to me, so the table would never feel empty at Thanksgiving, so I would never have the feeling of being poor of kin.

"The good thing about having three kids," I explained to Jennifer, "is that when they're older and one can't make it home for Thanksgiving for some reason, you're not just left with one measly kid."

"You don't really think like that, do you?"

"Yes," I clarified. "I do."

One of the things my children and I began doing together while Jennifer rested was watching nature shows. It was something that we all enjoyed, and as a parent, if you can find activities with your children that you also enjoy you're well ahead of the game; because inevitably some of the things they'll want you to do with them won't be so enjoyable, especially after the four hundred and fiftieth time. Children can be like Labrador retrievers in that they're drawn to repetition, as any parent who's played countless games of horsey ride or peekaboo will attest. But sitting on a comfortable couch with your children on your lap and watching the miracles of the animal kingdom can be so much more relaxing than actually having to get down on the carpet and be an animal, over and over and over again. Nature shows also seem to have a brilliant way of capturing the rhythms of life, from mating to birth to aging to death. They don't pull any punches when it comes to depicting the harshness of the animal world, and my first response was to want to cover Alex's and Nikki's eyes whenever some creature was about to be eaten, but after seeing gazelles get killed by cheetahs and yaks die of starvation they proved to me that they could accept death in a more matter-of-fact way than I could, and that there was really no reason to shelter them from it.

However, I did want to shelter them from seeing the death of a baby chimpanzee and the heartbroken expression on the mother's face as she continued to carry it around for days, even though it was dead.

One night we happened to see two rhinoceroses mating and it impressed me how gentle and attentive the enormous bull could be. Apparently, rhinoceroses take longer to copulate than almost any other animal, and according to the narrator, the reason they can take their time is that they have no enemies. It made me think: If deep down humans felt they had no enemies would they take longer to make love? Then, later that night, as I was heading up to bed, I tried to pretend that I was a rhinoceros without an enemy in the world. Including myself. And when I got into bed with Jennifer I felt an uncharacteristic calmness that I could only describe as being rhinoceros-like. I didn't even bother checking the doors to make sure they were locked, because there didn't seem to be any point for a rhinoceros to do this. I just snuggled up next to Jennifer and rested my face against her back, and while we didn't end up making love, I woke the next morning feeling as if we had, feeling the residue of closeness and peace that I had always associated with lovemaking.

17

EMBRACE
Conflict

THERE IS A DIFFERENCE between embracing conflict and picking a fight with someone you love. A lover embraces conflict. A bully or a helpless person picks a fight. And while picking a fight with your partner isn't something that I'd generally recommend, there are situations where more civilized discussions prove useless and yelling and screaming work better. However, if you and your partner find yourself arguing frequently about random things, you can be sure it's because there *are* emotions buried within both of you, since, on paper, a dish left on the counter or the thermostat turned down too low shouldn't be intensely emotional matters.

Self-involvement, though, can be an intensely emotional matter, particularly if it's as massive as an iceberg and is threatening to sink your relationship like an oversized passenger ship. Typically, most homes with a man around seem to have these icebergs to a greater or lesser extent, and this is because men have more of a tendency to think of themselves, while women have more of a tendency to think of everyone *but* themselves, which can make the journey of heterosexual love feel as choppy at times as a cruise on the *Titanic*. Not that homosexual relationships involve any smoother sailing from what I understand. I mean, in a gay relationship where there are two men, the likelihood of iceberg problems exponentially increase, and in a lesbian relationship, there is always the danger of some sort of caretaking meltdown. I, of course, am not an expert on homosexual relationships, being that I'm a straight man, but my sense from listening to my clients is that all couples fight over approximately the same thing: finding a format where both people can feel accepted, respected, empowered, and loved.

As I've mentioned before, it took a while for Rebecca and me to find the sibling version of this format, and a letter she wrote me in her early twenties seemed to accelerate this process. The gist of the letter was that she was tired of feeling unaccepted by me, tired of feeling inadequate as a sister, and had decided that if I couldn't find it in my heart to be a little more loving, then it would probably be better that we didn't have a lot to do with each other in the future. And the letter I wrote her back was anything but loving—I told her I was tired and pissed that she and my brother kept looking to get from me what they couldn't get from our parents—but over time our conflict seemed to lead to love. Not because we had necessarily solved anything. Not because we now had any more or less in common than before we wrote our letters. But more because we had confessed what we disliked about our relationship, and the result was that we were reminded of the truth that we really didn't hate each other.

I still give Rebecca credit for having the courage to take the first step, given how scary it can be to confess to someone you love what you hate about the relationship you have with them. As illogical as it is, you can almost feel that it's your fault for hating how they're treating you; and, of course, there are some people who will do all that they can to convince you that it *is* your fault, that you're being too sensitive or too demanding or too irrational, and even that what you're feeling has nothing to do with them, but instead has to do with people from your past, particularly your parents. This finger-pointing tactic is one that psychologists sometimes resort to in their personal lives in moments of cowardice, and if you happen to be in a relationship with a psychologist who says this to you, I wouldn't tolerate it for one second. I'd say, "Just cut it out, Mr. Clinical Man, and try being a person."

It seems that one of the keys to embracing conflict in a love-enhancing way is to realize that anything you do to tear down your partner also tears down your relationship. That is why all the variations of finger-pointing backfire. Psychological finger-pointing backfires. Moral finger-pointing backfires. And sexual finger-pointing backfires worst of all, because when someone is naked and open and reaching out for closeness the last thing they want or can tolerate is to be betrayed by their partner's judgments, by the accusations that they are this or they aren't that, which is different from saying that *we* don't have this or *we* don't have that. It is for this reason that when a couple has sexual problems it is usually a good idea that they see a therapist together, at least initially, rather than sending the person with performance or interest difficulties across town to have a specialist determine what is wrong with them.

And I have to admit that in Jennifer's initial stage of motherhood, when sex was of no more interest to her than blacktopping our driveway, I would have gladly sent her to a ginseng clinic or any specialist that I thought might bring an erotic twinkle back to her eye, but I knew it was something that we'd have to work out together, something that we'd have to work out over time. It is something to keep in mind when it comes to this business of embracing conflicts: sometimes we have to embrace them for a lot longer than what we'd ideally like. We can't just state the problem and expect it to be resolved by the next morning, no matter how much precious insight we might think we have. This is because most problems in relationships aren't due to a lack of insight. They are due more to habits of loving, habits that began long before any of us were of the age where we were interested in romantic partners.

Aside from the disagreement I had with my father about going to the Sadie Hawkins dance, I didn't really have any conflicts with my parents; instead, I just felt conflicted. It wasn't something that anyone could see on the outside. I was good in sports. I had friends. But I kept my emotional life to myself, which is what all of us end up doing when we choose to avoid conflicts with the people we love. Not that it really felt like a choice at the time. I knew my father was like a walking keg of dynamite, and that my mother was like a well of suffering, and I couldn't see how tossing my frustrations into the mix was going to help matters in my family. What seemed like a better idea was to keep myself *out* of the mix as much as possible, and yet when you keep yourself out of the mix of crucial relationships you begin to feel an isolation that is more chilling than having no relationships at all.

Of course, all of this felt normal at the time, and it was only when I began forming intimate relationships as a young man that I discovered you could have conflicts with someone you loved and that these conflicts could bring the two of you closer together. A conflict didn't have to destroy anyone. It didn't have to make anyone leave. Some conflicts could even involve humor, which isn't something I ever would have believed as a boy. At the time, all conflicts seemed to be about life and death, and I was quite certain that I didn't want to take a chance of dying, not physically or emotionally. I had seen my brother's gradual emotional death, and while I didn't think I could ever end up like him, I did worry that my anger might eventually erupt into violence.

However, the reality of anger seems to be that the harder we try to control it the more dangerous and out of control it feels. The most dangerous anger is the anger that has been stored the longest. A really old anger can sometimes damage a relationship so severely that it can never be repaired. I had a scary moment in my Restless Period when I feared that some old anger of mine had caused irreparable damage to our relationship, even though Jennifer never thought that the incident was as serious as I did. What happened was that I lost my temper because Jennifer insisted on doing a load of laundry on a Saturday night—instead of just hanging out together on the couch—and I threw a pillow at her head. While throwing a pillow at someone's head can be a funny thing to do under the right circumstances, the weight of the pillow and the emotions I felt while throwing it didn't make it funny in the least. The pillow was as round and dense as a basketball. We'd picked it up at her parents' furniture store, Charles Furniture Warehouse, located at 222 E. Harrison in charming Royal Oak, Michigan.

And in the moment that I threw it across the room I felt I had turned into my father.

The difference between my father and me was that I felt a sudden reflex to repair any damage that had occurred in my connection with Jennifer, while my father was prone to slipping into fits of silence that would feel more hurtful than whatever had caused him to be silent in the first place. And anyone who lives with a person, or was raised by a person, who is prone to such fits of silence can attest to how *violent* silence can be, how it can sever the relationship between two people in the cruelest way and leave the non-silent person with a wound so deep that it sometimes never heals. I remember I once worked with a woman who had such a wound, and in her case, she was plagued with the feeling that she didn't exist, which was a feeling I had trouble grasping at the time, but I think I can grasp it now, at least enough to appreciate how terrifying it can be to be faced with a void so powerful that it can overtake you.

What amazed me about this particular woman, and what

continues to amaze me about people like her, was how much she still appreciated life after having been through so much emotional and physical abuse. I suppose it is one of the things that still amazes me about my mother, even though this woman was a little funnier than my mother is. She was funny in the same outrageous way that Rebecca was funny. For example, when it came to the subject of silence in relationships, I remember her going on at length about how there should be shelters for domestic silence, just as there were shelters for domestic violence, and how overcrowded they'd be if there were such places, jam-packed with the partners of all sorts of *really* busy people, hugging folks they didn't know, weeping uncontrollably, wanting to play games they used to play as children.

As difficult as it can be to engage in conflicts with our partners, it can at times be even more difficult to engage in conflicts with our parents, no matter how old we are, no matter how many years it's been since they've been actively raising us. It seems our parents can always find a way to make us feel like children again. They can question if we're dressed warmly enough or if we've had enough to eat, and for a split second, we are transformed back into a nine-year-old kid. This can be a good feeling if it involves sweaters or soup; it can be a terrible feeling if it involves a judgment about how we're living our lives. And when our parents do something that makes us feel terrible—*anything* that makes us feel terrible—we really have no choice but to let them know about it. It doesn't matter if they're just visiting for the weekend. It doesn't matter if they're starting to show signs of age. We still have to let them know when they've hurt us if the love that's inside is going to keep coming out.

My father did something that hurt me after Rebecca died, or I should say that he did something that would have hurt Rebecca, and because it would have hurt Rebecca, it had a similar effect on me. Actually, what he did would have pissed Rebecca off more than hurt her, and I suppose that better describes how I was feeling when I got a flyer in the mail about the play he planned on producing at his humanistic synagogue in Rebecca's memory. To backtrack a little, my father has been putting on plays at humanistic synagogues and Jewish community centers for as long as I can remember, and it always bugged Rebecca that my father tried to relate to her as one writer to another, that he would try to involve her in conversations about "the stage" the way he would try to involve my brother and me in conversations about sports. In fairness to my father, it seemed to be his karma, as a parent of grown children, that he had to go out of his way to involve his kids in conversations with him, that it wasn't something they initiated.

"So I was thinking maybe you could send me a picture of Rebecca that I could use for the flyer," my father said when I called him to discuss his memorial play.

"You know, Rebecca wouldn't want you putting on a play in her memory," I reiterated.

"I feel a need to do something."

"Well, maybe you could do something that's more in line with the person that Rebecca was and the relationship that you had with her."

"I really didn't have much of a relationship with Rebecca," he said. "I mean, the truth is that she really didn't want to have anything to do with me."

"Then maybe a play in her memory would be a bit too much."

"I was the one who wanted to have a third child," he then told me. "I mean, your mother would have been happy to have had two, but I was the one who pushed for one more."

"What's the point?" I then asked, sensing that my mother would have a completely different account of all this.

"The point is that I lost a daughter, too. It's not just your mother. She's not the only one who's hurting."

"I didn't say she was the only one who was hurting."

"I mean, I didn't kill her, for chrissakes. I didn't tell her to go to Jamaica. I didn't tell her to get on a motorcycle. So I don't see why everyone's blaming me for this."

"No one's blaming you," I clarified.

"No, *you* blame me—and so does your mother. I can tell. I could tell at the funeral, that you were both thinking that if I had been a better father to her then none of this would have happened."

"That's not true," I said, then stopped to consider if it really was true.

"This isn't how I wanted things to turn out. Don't you understand? I never wanted to have a wife leave me or a son who hates me or a daughter who dies before I do. I mean, I wanted the same things when I was starting out that you want for your family right now. That's what no one seems to understand about what happened in the past—

that I hated what was going on as much as anyone. I just didn't know what to do about it. Once things started going bad there seemed to be no way to get them to go good again."

"I don't hate you, Dad," I told him, and I found myself wishing we were having this conversation in person instead of by phone where I couldn't see his face or reach out and touch him.

"I suppose I could go ahead and do the play without putting her picture on the program."

"I said, I don't hate you," I repeated, feeling my heart pounding as the words came out of me.

"That's good to hear, son," he concluded. "Because you're the one person I couldn't take hating me right now."

18

SHOP WITH
Your Partner

IT IS A MUCH DIFFERENT EXPERIENCE to shop with
your partner than it is to shop alone. I suppose it is a
different experience to do *anything* with your partner than
to do it alone, and when I was in my Restless Period I had
trouble appreciating how different these two experiences
could be. It seems to be one of the hallmarks of restlessness: that you have trouble appreciating togetherness no
matter how hard you try. And maybe one of the truths
about Restless People is that they really don't try that hard
at it, that their urgency to get somewhere or do something
precludes any possible camaraderie that might be involved
in the process. And one thing that I'd do if I were a shopping mall owner is to do a better job of promoting the
camaraderie of shopping. I'd show mothers shopping with
daughters and fathers shopping with sons and friends
shopping with friends. The theme of my advertising cam-
paign would be You Can Feel Love in the Mall. You can
feel it walking across the parking lot on a hot and muggy
day. You can feel it when a store has a sale that excites

both of you. Isn't it nice when you and your partner get excited about the same thing? I suppose it is more than nice. I suppose it is essential.

A shopping mall is also a good place to forget about death for a while. You can go to one of these vast places with its fountains and countless stores and not have to think about who you've lost and who you might eventually lose, including yourself, which is kind of a weird thing to think about losing, particularly when you consider that you won't even be able to think about your not being here when you're gone. No brain for thinking. No hands for touching. It is hard to imagine letting go of all that and becoming a microscopic soap bubble floating in space, floating out in a realm where there are no Chinese restaurants or gyms or bookstores. It is especially hard to imagine having to say good-bye to all the people you love, as well as some of the people who are a part of your life in a much smaller way, like the neighbors who you wave to in passing, like the friendly woman who works at the People's Food Co-op on Wednesday. Death definitely must be an incredible adjustment period, no longer being able to shop for your favorite foods, no longer being able to stick your toes in a cool fountain on a hot summer day.

Or maybe it isn't such an adjustment after all. I think it was John Lennon who said that he expected death to be kind of like getting out of one taxicab and getting into another.

But when death is on your mind, when it is part of your consciousness, you can think about it anywhere, even at a shopping mall. You can see a pair of shoes in a store and say to your partner, "My sister would have liked these." And when a salesperson overhears you, or thinks he overhears you, and replies, "Maybe you could buy them for her," you are then in a position where you have to tell the clerk that your sister died. You have to enlist that person as a witness. It all happens in the process of someone trying to sell you a pair of shoes. What surprises you is that the salesperson wants to know *how* she died. You are taken by the clerk's curiosity, and so you explain how she had just finished a screenplay and went to Jamaica to celebrate and ended up getting killed when a truck hit a motorcycle she was driving.

"I'm sorry, man," the clerk says as the manager walks by to make sure we're getting the shoes we need.

DO YOU HAVE good shopping memories from your childhood? I ask this because I can't really seem to come up with any. What I can remember about shopping with my parents is that they tried to spend as little time as possible doing it and then having these pained looks on their faces whenever they discovered the price of anything. It was as if price tags were their enemies, and since I was a child, I guess it also felt that what I wanted was their enemy, too. So I learned to want less. Children can teach themselves to do that, and those that do tend not to grow up to be very fun shopping partners as adults. It is the indulgent aspect of shopping that can be most frightening to those of us with this kind of shopping disability, because if we allow ourselves to feel this pleasure as adults it forces us to come to grips with how the withholding of this pleasure might have hurt us as children.

And a couple's financial situation isn't necessarily the most critical variable in how indulgent they are with each other or themselves. There are poor people who are generous. There are rich people who are stingy. And almost all people who are stingy with their money are also stingy with their hearts. Can you think of an exception? I can't. What I can think of instead are a number of individuals who believe that if they save their love and their time they will be richer. This, of course, isn't true. It's an illusion, just as it's an illusion that it uses energy—and costs money—to make ice cubes in your own freezer. That used to be my father's rationale for recycling ice cubes, for taking them out of his glass when he was finished with his drink and putting them back into the cube trays. Needless to say, it was a practice of his that made me feel like a member of the Loser Family.

Another thing my father did—and my mother accepted— that made me feel like a member of the Loser Family was to staple my shoes when I wore a hole through them. Actually, it made me feel less like a member of the Loser Family and more just like a Loser Boy. The black adhesive he used to fix my shoes had the same effect. It was some kind of glue that was probably intended for plumbing repair. I remember the smell of it made me sick to my stomach, and even long after the smell was gone, I would look down at my patched-up shoes and feel a terrible nausea.

This all happened in a middle-class neighborhood where other kids wore Keds and Hush Puppies and Red Ball Jets and PF Flyers. It didn't happen in a Polish orphanage.

But one of the advantages of being an adult is that you can treat yourself to something nice when you're feeling a need to be treated. Or you can let yourself be treated to something nice by your partner, assuming that your partner's the giving type, which hopefully is the case; because if not, you could end up feeling the way I did when my father would staple my shoes. And I must admit that I've made myself feel this way before by being too cheap with myself, as if life were a contest to see who could want the least. Can't life really suck when we treat ourselves the way we hated being treated by our parents? I know it's been helpful for me to go shopping with Jennifer instead of on my own, and this might be something that would be helpful to anyone with a similar kind of shopping disability. Sometimes you just need someone who isn't you to get you to be nicer to yourself.

In a nutshell, that might be a good way to describe psychotherapy.

If you're a parent, you might also find that buying stuff for your kids can help heal some wounds caused by frugality. I know I have bought my own kids more pairs of Nike, Fila, Adidas, Reebok, Pro-Keds, and Converse shoes than shoe reps probably buy for their children. I buy them shoes almost out of defiance, and yet I must admit that seeing them with a perfect pair of high-tops on their feet does touch something in me. It makes me feel excited and proud and sad all at once. There was a time I even gave serious consideration to opening up an athletic shoe store instead of studying to become a psychologist, but then it occurred to me that I didn't want to be in the business of selling shoes; I really wanted to give them away, to be a broker of athletic shoes to disadvantaged kids, to be the ultimate Good Dad of Shoes, which is still something I might someday do if the foundation gods see fit.

I forgot to mention one other thing about the day Jennifer and I went to the mall for our date, and that is that the money I had on me was from the check my mother had given us from Rebecca's return flight. Our mini-shopping spree was compliments of Rebecca. Only I wasn't doing much in the way of spreeing. For some reason, I just couldn't seem to get my side of the spree off the ground. I tried to explain to Jennifer that there wasn't anything I really needed, and she encouraged me to try and think in terms of what I *wanted*. This made me uncomfortable. I felt like a rank beginner when it came to wanting, and it didn't help that all the clothes I tried on at the Gap (is there a mall in the universe that doesn't have a Gap?) seemed as if they were made for someone much taller and skinnier than me. The Gap clothes made me feel old. They made me feel a part of a lineage of hairy, muscular, Eastern European oxcart pullers.

After we left the Gap, I asked myself how Rebecca would want me to spend the money, which led me back to the shoe store where I had told the young clerk the story of how she died. He was still there, and we shook hands, as if we were old friends. He was a light-skinned African American man, and as we began talking, he mentioned that his grandmother was from Jamaica and that he hoped to visit there someday. I made him promise that he would stay away from motorcycles if he did; it was a promise that I sometimes wished everyone would make, including all the Harley riders who were so passionate about their bikes. The world just didn't seem to need motorcycles or people riding them.

I then tried on a pair of hiking boots and it choked me up to think that this would be Rebecca's last stand on earth, buying her older brother a pair of hiking boots. It made me wonder if the boots would ever feel like just a pair of boots, or if they would always feel like a connection with her. A part of me felt reluctant to even wear them, felt like keeping them in a glass case so they would last forever, and yet I knew a person can't live like that. I knew that what would give the shoes the most life was for me to live as passionately as possible while they were on my feet.

19

DO LESS

Out of Obligation

I'M NOT SUGGESTING being selfish. In fact, I'm suggesting just the opposite: give more to others, but give more out of desire and less out of a sense of duty. Because duty doesn't seem to work well when it is the essence of a relationship; as the essence, it just doesn't seem to yield love. What it can lead to instead is a nagging resentment that can get so thick it smothers just about any desire. This holds true both in and out of the bedroom.

It even holds true after your sister dies when you find yourself calling your mother because you feel an obligation to be there for her in her grief, especially after she mentioned the week before that you and your family were *all* she had, that you're what kept her going, that if it weren't for you she probably wouldn't be here. You don't know how to take this. You know it was said out of love. You know it was meant to express your specialness to her. But it doesn't feel good to be *all* that someone has. It feels heavy. It makes you feel less free. And you want to know why others aren't included in this all-she-has club. Like her friends.

Like her husband. After all, they'd been married for four-teen years. It wasn't like they just met. It wasn't like he screamed about lights being left on the way my father did. He, my stepfather, Marv, is a nice man. But maybe he isn't a Good Death Man. Because he did go to work the next morning after Rebecca died and that's not something a Good Death Man would do. A Good Death Man always stays with death. He holds its hand as if it were a child. So was this my mother's karma? To be married to one man who wasn't good with marriage and another man who wasn't good with death? And this leaves you feeling like a son who has to be good with *everything*, especially at staying alive. You know it would send your mother over the edge if something happened to you. She has come right out and said this. But you're not quite sure how you go about being better at staying alive, how you make sure that you end up well above the mean. Because death is not like a GRE. You can't just take a Stanley Kaplan class for it. You can wear seat belts and eat organic plums, but there is no guarantee that will be enough. And then one magical winter day your children want to walk across a frozen pond and you don't know what to tell them. A part of you feels like saying, "We have become the People Who Are Afraid of Death and this is no longer something we can do." But there are other children walking across the pond with their parents. There is a group of boys playing hockey. And you don't want your children to be afraid of life. So you take their hands and step out onto the ice and you can't recall a day where the sky ever looked clearer. The whole pond seems to glow from the brightness of the sun. Then you make the mistake of trying to share this experience with your mother, of trying to tell her how wonderful it was to be out with the other families and have the thick ice support you, but you can tell it is too much for her.

"You shouldn't take chances," she said, her voice trembling.

"I wasn't taking chances. There were other people out there with us, people even playing hockey."

"But those other people aren't my son, they're not my family."

"We can't stop living, Mom," I then said to her, and I felt bad that so much of life still frightened her.

"I know we can't," she agreed, and we then made plans of when we'd see each other next before ending our conversation and hanging up the phone.

Does it ever seem that it gets harder to say no as we get older? I bring this up because children seem to say no so effortlessly. It flows right out of their mouths without hesitation. I'll ask our kids if they'll help me pull up some weeds in the front yard and they'll just say, "No, Dad, I don't want to." (It still is a mystery to me how some vegetation gets classified as plants and are lovingly cared for like little babies, while other vegetation gets classified as weeds and are treated like the devil.) They don't worry about me attacking them. They don't worry about me leaving them. I assume they would help me weed if they did, because no child wants to be attacked or left by their parents. It is much safer for a child to betray their own desires—in this case, the desire *not* to weed—and yet in the long run that isn't a very safe thing to do either.

Because if we betray our desires long enough they will eventually betray us back. They will betray us by running away or hiding, and then we will become a Person with Hidden Desires. I see People with Hidden Desires all the time in my practice. Most of them look and act just about the same as anyone else. They wear shirts with sailboats or polo horses on them. They drive well-made cars. They have friends over for dinner and serve wine with grilled fish. But then they have moments during the day when it occurs to them: I don't really love anything; I just do things that I think I *should* be doing, things that people do who are successful or helpful or responsible or ambitious or hardworking.

I hope it doesn't sound as if I'm in any way making fun (i.e., references to nautical clothing and grilled fish) of People with Hidden Desires, because it is always a painful condition; only it is a *dull* pain, and that is sometimes why the person suffering from it isn't motivated to take action. This is true of other dull pains: they are often bearable enough to forgo intervention or treatment. I'm reminded of a question from a licensing exam I took a number of years back, which was: What is one of the most critical variables for success in psychotherapy? The answer wasn't how well-trained the therapist was or how many times a week the client was in therapy. The answer was how *miserable* the client was, because apparently when we're *really* miserable we're motivated to do something about our situation in a way that we're not when we're only kind of miserable.

Getting back to how some people might act out of ob-

ligation so others won't leave, I should add that usually
when someone leaves it's not a physical thing, meaning
they don't pick themselves up and head out the door—
though that kind of leaving can happen, too. Usually, when
they leave they do it more emotionally. It's one of those
things where they're there, but they're not really there;
they're somewhere inside themselves. That's what can
make it so hard to chase after them. I mean, if they took
off out the back door, you could at least run after them
and tackle them by the waist. But it is hard to tackle someone by the waist who is withdrawn, because most withdrawn people don't want to be touched. Some don't even
want to *admit* they're withdrawn. That can really make you
feel crazy—when someone's gone and they insist that
they're still there. There was even a time when psychologists thought that schizophrenia was caused by mothers
who did this (i.e., the schizophrenogenic mother).

I suppose there was a time when psychologists thought
that *everything* was caused by mothers who did or didn't do
something.

As for my children not wanting to help me weed the
front yard, I'll tell you something that happens more often
than not: they come out and join me once they don't feel
they have to. It's a funny phenomenon, how when we feel
we have to do something we no longer want to do it, even
if it's something we normally would want to do. I know it's
a phenomenon that can affect the sex lives of some couples,
and when it does, it's never really funny for either of them.
It's been my experience that few things are as unfunny as
feeling sexually disconnected from your partner, and yet I

realize not everyone is like me, a man who is probably more in the camp of People with Overwhelming Desires than the camp of People with Hidden Desires. (I'm convinced there is a camp somewhere in the middle there.) And I can't help but think of what a female friend once said to me in college: Sex is only important when you're not having it or when you're having it and it's bad.

But just as my children found themselves more interested in weeding—or in being with me—once they felt off the hook, I found myself more interested in being with my mother once I felt this was no longer something I was obligated to do, once I accepted that she was strong enough to handle the disappointment of me not being there for her—which isn't to say that she *was* disappointed, but rather that this was what I expected her to be. And a lot of what we do out of obligation seems to be because we expect that people will feel a certain way if we don't do it. We expect they will feel resentful, we expect they will feel devastated, and then we hurry around like busboys so they won't feel this way, until it occurs to us how impossible it is to love someone we view as that fragile. This is because love is an inherently rigorous activity. It involves steep terrain. It involves inclement weather. And when we're about to embark on its trail we need to feel that we're with someone who is capable of carrying their own weight.

For the longest time, I never felt I could love my brother because he seemed so fragile, and yet he showed that he could handle Rebecca's death much better than a truly fragile person ever could. He didn't get lost in the past, producing a stream of letters about family events from the '60s and '70s, and he didn't seem to have a need to build me up to be everything that he wasn't. This was all a change. It was a change that I appreciated when we met for lunch about once a month, because when you're in a Chinese restaurant and life feels uncertain the last thing you want is your older brother to treat you like you were the Michael Jordan of your family. You just want him to treat you like a person, to treat you like a brother, so that way you might be able to figure out how to love him.

"Do you sometimes think about how if Hitler never attacked Poland then we probably wouldn't be here?" Ezra asked. "Because then Mom never would have left and gone to Israel and she never would have met Dad, and everything would have just turned out different for everyone."

"You could have been the leading scorer of Poland's national basketball team," I kidded him; there once was a time, many years ago, when we played a lot of basketball together.

"I never had the nerves to be a scorer. You had the nerves. Maybe little Alex will be that way, too. Maybe he won't let the pressure get to him."

"I bought them a little basketball hoop that we keep in the toy room. They play all the time."

"I hope you and Jennifer have another child," Ezra said, and I could tell it was something that had been on his mind. "Do you think you will?"

"Maybe. I'm not really sure."

"I think it would be good for everyone," he then said

and went on to explain how if we had a third child it would replace him in the world in the same way that Nikki and Alex would eventually replace Rebecca and me.

I imagined it would probably be good for my mother if we had another child, and yet I knew that parents had to have children for themselves, that doing it for someone else—even for your spouse—almost always backfires in a profound way, as all intensely effortful undertakings do when they're done out of obligation. I mean, can you imagine what it'd be like to devote yourself to a career because you think it'd make someone else happy? That surely would lead to a big dose of misery, and it always does for those who choose a profession because they think it will please their parents. It is much better for people in that situation to agree to take out their parents' trash and mow their lawn for the next thirty years than to sacrifice their entire professional life. And while you might be able to *undo* an unwise career choice, the same isn't true of parenthood. You can't leave your children the way you can leave medical school, at least not without hurting them a great deal. There is no way to get around the truth: Children get hurt when they're left. They get hurt no matter how the leaving is explained or what they're given as compensation.

Maybe the reality is that we all get hurt when we're left. Six months after Rebecca's death, that still seemed to be my mother's truth. I knew it was her truth, even though we didn't talk as much on the phone, even if I didn't come over as often with the children for weekend visits. And I could tell she had reached a decision in her mind that she needed to start giving me more *space*, that it might have been okay to rely on me more intensely during the initial months of bereavement, but that I was a grown man who had his own life, and that she couldn't expect me to live through Rebecca's death with her. And what I felt like telling her was, "Yes, Mom, I do have my own life, but that doesn't mean our lives have to be completely separate. That doesn't mean I can't live through *some* of Rebecca's death with you. I just can't be the only one who helps you through this, just as you could never be the only one who helps me through such a tragic loss. Because I really don't think space has to be an all-or-nothing thing, and quite frankly, Mom, I think space is overrated. I think it is what we ask for when we don't know how to ask for other things. So what I'm asking from you, Mom, is that we keep trying to find that balance between having our own lives and having a common life, a common life that is precious even though it has its limitations."

Often when I visited my mother I took advantage of the opportunity to sit on the couch in front of a televised sports event and do absolutely nothing, which Jennifer thought was rude, but which my mother accepted and even encouraged. She always said that she wanted me to be able to relax when I came to visit, and there *was* something incredibly relaxing about curling up on her womblike leather couch and watching Barry Sanders do things that I once dreamed of being able to do when I was a grown man. In part, what made the experience so relaxing was knowing that the two women who were most a part of me—Jennifer and my mother—were giving our children all the love and attention they needed, which gave me the feeling that indirectly I was giving them all the love and attention they needed, only I didn't have to get off the couch.

In many respects, it was every parent's fantasy come true: a moment where you can enjoy your love for your children without them being able to demand anything from you.

I was watching a Bulls-Knicks game at my mother's house one Sunday when she entered the room and said she was going out for a while. Alex was napping, and Jennifer and her mother had taken Nikki to see *The Lion King*, and I was on the couch, as usual, watching Michael Jordan single-handedly torch the Knicks to the dismay of Spike Lee and the rest of the fans at the Garden. For some reason, as I saw Spike Lee waving a towel on the sidelines, it made me recall how Rebecca once told me that he grew up rich, which isn't to say that he shouldn't have grown up rich, but more to point out how I began recalling other things she had told me over the years: that most of the people in her African dance class were Jewish; that it seemed so funny to her that there were now so many different kinds of mustard; that if she could go fishing with anyone in the world, past or present, it would be Albert Einstein.

"So where are you going?" I asked my mother, turning down the volume of the TV.

"I'm going to the cemetery," she said.

"I'll go with you, if you can wait until Alex wakes up."

"I should probably go by myself," she replied unconvincingly.

"You can go by yourself another time," I insisted. "Just wait twenty minutes and we'll all go together."

"Okay," she agreed, and as soon as Alex woke up from his nap, I changed his diaper, dressed him in his winter coat, and we headed to the cemetery.

It was strange being at the cemetery with Alex. I looked at him running across the grass and he seemed the antithesis of death. His cheeks alone seemed the antithesis of death, so round and full of life, similar to how Jennifer's were when she was younger. I thought to myself, "Life cheeks," and kept playing these words over and over in my mind. I then looked at my mother who was kneeling by the grave marker and weeping and these words left my mind. The word *daughterless* took their place. It sounded like such a strange word, so strange that it felt like I had just made it up. I couldn't recall ever hearing anyone use the word. But it was a word that seemed to best describe my mother as she wept on her knees beside Rebecca's grave. Maybe it was a word that best described any mother who lost her girl. I took Alex in my arms and went up and sat behind my mother, so she could lean her back against mine. We looked in opposite directions without saying anything. I gave Alex a pretzel and the only sounds were of his munching and of the breeze blowing through the trees. I had never sat with my mother's back against mine, and yet it felt surprisingly comfortable, each of us helping to support the other.

"We'll have to pick out a tombstone soon for the unveiling," she said as we stood up and headed for the car.

"When's that?" I asked.

"In six months—about a year after the funeral."

"Can I ask you a question?" I then said. "I know it has nothing to do with the unveiling, but were you still in Poland when the Nazis invaded?"

"Yes," she told me. "Our apartment was actually bombed by the German army in the middle of the night. I can remember having to jump out of the second-story window onto broken glass and being afraid and my mother screaming, 'Jump, jump.' "

"That must have been terrifying."

"Strangely enough, do you know what was most terrifying? It wasn't the bombs or the fires or the tanks, it was the sound of the soldiers' boots as they marched through the street. That was more terrifying to me than anything."

With my left arm around her, holding Alex with my right, I whispered, "I'm sorry," because I was sorry that she had had to go through that, sorry that this haunting memory was still with her, and sorry that she had to think of it in a cemetery where her daughter was buried.

20

APPRECIATE

The Big Moments

BIRTH AND DEATH almost seem to demand our appreciation, but the rest of the moments—the in-between moments—tend to be more reserved. It's as if they're content to blend in with other moments, and some moments can blend in so well that you barely notice them. Actually, when you notice them most is not when they're there, but when they're gone. This is when my father began appreciating all the moments he had with my mother and our family— after they came to a screeching halt.

Sentimental people often do this, often make a big deal about a moment long after they've had the opportunity to be in it. It's common for a man to act this way with his daughter, to be busy in his studies or workshops for the majority of her girlhood and adolescence (particularly after puberty) and then to get all syrupy and bent out of shape when she reaches the dating age and is ready to have a life of her own. One thing I promised myself when I became a parent was that I'd try to get excited about being with my children at the same time when they were excited about

being with me. It was helpful for me to look at my relationships with them as a checking account, with the idea
that the more loving moments I invested in their accounts
early on, the more love and friendship I'd be able to draw
from them as they got older and I got older.

This isn't to say that a parent and a child can't invest
big moments (i.e., loving moments) in their accounts when
they're both adults, even though they won't have the benefit
of accruing interest as they would if they'd begun when the
child was young. And there is always the chance that a child
will grow up and lose interest in having a joint account
with a parent, as Rebecca did with my father. She simply
decided that it would be better for her if they did their
banking separately; but I shouldn't say "simply," since it
is probably never really simple when we give up trying to
have an involved relationship with one of our parents. The
same is probably true to a lesser extent in any relationship;
it hurts to throw in the towel, to look in the mirror and
confess, "I don't think I can have any more loving moments with this person."

Are loving moments the same as big moments? While
being a psychologist doesn't necessarily make me an expert
on moments, I'd have to say that all loving moments are
big moments—but that all big moments aren't loving moments. An example of a big moment that wasn't a loving
moment for my mother was the sound of the Nazis marching through the streets of Warsaw. Anything you remember
many years later is a big moment, because it indicates that
the moment has left its mark on you, that it changed you
in some way, which is what *all* big moments do.

This means that some moments might appear to be big to us at the time, while others might not appear big until years later when we're able to look back on them. The advantage of appreciating big moments in the present is that we might be able to change our lives in such a way as to create more of them. While the notion of creating big moments might sound contrived, I think this is one of the main reasons we seek out loving relationships: they tend to create more big moments than when we're by ourselves. Some loving relationships can become almost like big-moment factories, and I suppose this is one of the aspects of falling in love that is so intoxicating, that big moments keep rolling off the production line practically every day, practically every hour.

Then some couples find that over time the production of big moments slows down and even comes to a halt. This doesn't have to happen. Big moments don't have to be confined to the first years of a relationship or a marriage, as some cynical people—mostly men—insist they do; and yet big moments, both sexual and nonsexual, will surely end as soon as we start feeling entitled to them, as soon as we find ourselves sitting on our thrones demanding that they appear. That is the difference between life and pornography. In pornography, entitled men are blessed with big moments in the most erotic and magical way, and yet in real life, the entitled man's lack of humility, his lack of appreciation for the preciousness of life, usually restricts the size of his moments to an evening spent with a *Playboy* magazine and a six-pack of Bud Light.

I know, because when I was in my Restless Period,

when I was feeling as entitled as Henry VIII, I was about to skim through a *Playboy* magazine that a basketball buddy had sent me (he said, "This is what a guy like *you* needs") when I did something that most *Playboy* subscribers probably never do: I picked up a copy of my wife's *Ms.* magazine. And I began reading an article about men who were seeking big and magical moments for themselves by going on "sex junkets" to Thailand, and the more I read, the less interested I was in picking up the *Playboy* and taking a meaningless glance at pictures of naked women who weren't my wife, because it occurred to me that the *Playboy* models, as happy and glamorous and energetic as they were intended to appear, were cousins of those same girls in Thailand who were enslaved—literally enslaved—into prostitution, and that if you were truly going to have a big moment or a magical moment, it couldn't be at the expense of someone else having a dehumanizing moment, particularly if that someone is a girl of thirteen.

A sex tip for all men, particularly those considering going on a "sex junket" to Thailand: Read *Ms.* magazine.

As for those *other* big moments, the unloving moments, like what my mother went through when the Nazi soldiers marched through the streets of her neighborhood, I prefer to think that even they offer some opportunity for growth, as idealistic a notion as this might be. A Christian client of mine often says that "God never gives you more than you can handle" and "what doesn't break you makes you stronger," and I would like to believe there is truth in both these statements, even though most of us can think of instances where God *does* give people more than they can handle. He seemed to do this with Ezra, who, for whatever reason, didn't come to this earth wired as a survivor. Because most survivors have a keen ability to hate what is happening to them, to see themselves pitted *against* what is happening to them, which isn't an ability that Ezra ever had; and while it is an ability that both my mother and I have, I don't think it is possible to grow from past big moments by continuing to feel hate, by continuing to hold the position of being *against* something.

That is why I thought it would be good for my mother to tell her story to the Shoah Foundation, because if she told it honestly, if she appreciated the power of her early experiences and how helpless she and the rest of humanity were in the face of Nazism, then maybe her story would heal her in the same way that telling the story of Rebecca's death seemed to heal me. After all, wasn't this how people healed themselves in psychotherapy, by telling their story as honestly as they could, telling it over and over and over again, and as their story gradually changed over time, as it became more compassionate and forgiving and loving, they too changed?

What was the story of Rebecca's death? I asked myself this question one day in my office, and while I was well aware of her story's ending, I had trouble coming up with its meaning, because it still didn't seem to have much meaning that she died, at least not in the sense that all the changes that Jennifer and I went through couldn't have been made with her living, with her calling from New York and coming to visit on holidays. I mean, she didn't have to die just so Jennifer and I could appreciate our love for each other. I'm sure it could have happened in some other way. Just getting a better feel of the balance between parenthood and marriage probably would have helped. Or something could have shocked us. Something like a *near* car accident where you have to lock up your brakes and nearly hit a tree and are reminded of how short life can be. Was Rebecca's life really short? I guess the fact that mine was longer made it seem this way, made it seem as if she hadn't lived a complete life, but had only lived a part of her life; and yet the truth is that we all live a complete life, *our* complete life, that we find a way to come full circle.

But it was still hard for me to imagine how Rebecca did that at the age of twenty-eight on a motorcycle that was hit by a truck in Jamaica. I tend to think of coming full circle as something that happens under more peaceful circumstances, like on a beach at sunset or on a garden terrace late at night; but since Rebecca didn't live all that peacefully, maybe it isn't fair to expect that she would have died this way. I have heard the expression more than once that we die the way we live, which seems as good a wake-up call as any of us need to live a more loving life.

And I emphasize a *loving* life, because I once knew a man who came close to death, who suffered a stroke and looked death straight in the eyes, and he said the *only* thing that was of comfort to him in that moment on the edge was love, love he felt from his family and friends, love he felt *for* them, just love swirling around him, swirling and swirling.

I then closed my eyes and thought I might try taking a

nap, but before I could fall asleep, I had the strangest experience, an experience I feel funny even telling you out of fear that you'll think I'm crazy, crazy in a New Age sort of way. What happened as I closed my eyes was that I had the clearest image of Rebecca's face against a blue background, a bright blue background, like the brightest blue sky you've ever seen, and at first it scared me—terrified me—because it didn't feel like a dream or anything I could control, but then I slowed myself down and just looked at it, looked at her, and felt comforted by how peaceful she seemed, totally peaceful, the way I often hoped she would be. And after she went away I felt a strange calmness that I can barely put into words. It is the kind of calmness you might feel if you trusted that everything in your life would work out in the end, maybe not exactly how you thought it might, but in some way that felt destined and meaningful.

It was a calmness that I couldn't recall ever feeling before.

"Come visit me again, sis," I whispered, reaching for a necklace of hers that I kept on an end table. "Come visit me whenever you can."

21

MAKE LOVE
On Wednesday

I FEEL FUNNY telling people when they should make love. I mean, half the time I don't even know when Jennifer and I should make love. During my Restless Period, I was convinced that we should make love every other day, as if lovemaking was similar to weight training; this was at a time when I felt a need to have a schedule for all of our family activities. A schedule for baths. A schedule for meals. A schedule for relaxing conversation. It was stupid, and yet stupidity seems to be an inherent part of parenting. I could write a trilogy of the stupid things that Jennifer and I have tried in an attempt to get our children to do what we want. There was a period when Nikki couldn't fall asleep without sucking a frozen banana. Yes, a frozen banana. In retrospect, supplying a child with a frozen banana seems like something that only parents on an acid trip would do—or maybe parents who can't bear the sound of their own child crying.

It can be so hard to disappoint the people we love.

And I could probably also write a trilogy of the stupid things that Jennifer and I did as partners when we were in a rut, including going to sleep at different times. It is almost always a strain on a relationship when two people have drastically different schedules. It can be such a strain that you and your partner can end up feeling as if you're not the same species, which is never a good feeling. I mean, imagine how senseless and lonely it would feel for a cougar who was trying to create a life together with a wolf. From what I've heard about cougars, life probably feels senseless and lonely for them anyway, given that they tend to isolate themselves for months at a stretch and then compensate for this by copulating up to seventy times a day when they come across a suitable mate.

Does it feel as if you and your partner are living like this, isolating yourselves throughout the work week, and then trying to make up for it on one spectacular Saturday night? If it does, you might want to try reaching out to each other on a Wednesday or Thursday, even making a "love date" or a "cuddle date" or just a "being together date." I know you're probably thinking that this suggestion would be a wonderful addition to my stupid things trilogy, that a sensual connection needs to be as spontaneous as play, and yet we *do* make dates for other kinds of play. We make golf dates and tennis dates, not knowing at the time how passionate we will be feeling when we're out on the course or court; and yet we trust that we will feel passionate enough to make it worthwhile, that putting ourselves in a passionate place will increase the chance of passion emerging.

Because the reality is that if we don't commit ourselves to an opportunity for closeness and sensuality then we will eventually commit ourselves to something else, something like an investment group or a committee on brief psycho-therapy where pie charts and bar graphs are flashed before us on a screen and we head home at nine or ten at night with much less love swirling around us, putting ourselves at risk for the most frightening of deaths: a pie chart–bar graph death involving an employer's money. That was one of the reasons I quit my job at the Big Medical Center: I could feel pie charts and bar graphs swirling around me. They were swirling around me even though I never vol-unteered to be on a committee for brief, or cost-effective, psychotherapy, even though I was just a responsible family man breathing the corporate air.

And if you happen to be going for an initial appoint-ment with a therapist who has shelves of books of brief psychotherapy and a posting for the next World Conference on Brief and Cost-Effective Psychotherapy—like a therapist who was assigned to you by your friendly HMO provider—my advice would be to get up from your chair and run like hell, because there is a good chance that your therapist might try to get you to lose interest in your emotional life within three to five sessions. They could even diagnose you as having a borderline personality disorder if you don't lose interest, if you want to continue to have a therapeutic re-lationship, if it hurts too much to say good-bye. Then they might want to put you in a group with other people who have trouble saying good-bye, with other people who want to have love swirling around them. The only problem is that the group probably won't last very long either (i.e., it will be a "time-limited" group) and then you'll find yourself having to say more good-byes, both to your group brothers and sisters, as well as the new therapist.

This isn't to say that there is anything wrong with a time-limited group, or time-limited psychotherapy, just as long as you, the client, have some input into what the limits of time will be. It reminds me of an incident in high school where three friends and I went to a greasy spoon restaurant advertising "All You Can Eat Spaghetti—$3.95," and after two plates each, the disgruntled owner came out of the kitchen and said, "That's all you can eat." We, of course, had a different interpretation of his all-you-can-eat special and refused to pay our bill unless he agreed to send more spaghetti our way. He ended up calling the police, and they came and sided with us, saying he had to either give us unlimited spaghetti access right then or a rain check for another meal's worth of spaghetti.

I suppose it'd be nice if our relationships had the equivalent of all-you-can-eat specials. Like on Monday you could have all the compassion you wanted and then Saturday might be your day for unlimited affection. Then maybe on Tuesdays you could go for sensual touch and on Thursdays for smiles and laughter. However, the reality of a relationship is that our partners have limits, just as we have limits, and in the course of loving each other there will be moments when each of you will have to come out of the kitchen like a disgruntled restaurant owner and say, "That's enough. I have no more to give you." And, unfortunately (or fortunately), when this happens there will be no police for either of you to call, no one to come in and mediate the crisis. It will be the two of you who will have to figure out how to get more spaghetti or more openness or whatever it is that is in short supply.

A common thing that many couples find is in short supply in their relationship is time together, which makes everything seem as if it's in short supply. You and your partner can have wonderful communication and wonderful this and wonderful that, but it's not going to add up to much if you're spending all your time apart. Despite the "efficiency" of life in the age of technological advances, one thing has remained unchanged: Love still takes time.

Also, when I refer to making love, I don't just mean in the traditional sense, but rather in terms of any act that makes or creates a feeling of love. This could include meeting for lunch, even though that's not equated with love-making in most people's minds. However, there is something fun about seeing your partner in the middle of the day, providing your schedules allow for this. It can feel like recess, or even hooky, which is something I never played. I was always too afraid of getting caught. But who can catch us as adults except our own notions of work and responsibility and ambition? And what can happen even if we do get caught? Will we get sent to the principal's office? Will we be forced to spend a few days at home? Will we be made to feel guilty?

I'll tell you what Dr. Bob once said about guilt: it's anger dressed in drag. And what he meant by this is that in every situation where someone feels guilty they could just as easily feel angry (or hurt) if they stepped back and took a different perspective. An example of this is a person who feels guilty for being sexual could also be angry about being raised in a home where it was taught that sex was wrong and dirty—or even raised in a home where physical affection was absent.

Another example of this is a person, my mother, who felt guilty that she couldn't insulate Rebecca from some of the loneliness and insecurity and fear that she'd experienced as a child, but at the same time felt that she'd had no such insulation in her own childhood. A childhood without insulation: that's what my mother had. A childhood with firebombs. A childhood with soldiers marching. So what did she expect of herself? To be waiting for us in the kitchen like Betty Crocker when we came home from school? To be drawn toward a gentle man? It was almost more logical to be drawn toward a man whose rage was on the outside, so that she could fight it in a way that would have been impossible had it remained inside herself. She could once again have something to be against, which, as I've already mentioned, is what a survivor needs, or at least what feels most natural. But was that my mother's fault? Did she start a family with the intention of re-creating the horror of her childhood? Of course she didn't, and of course we were much better off than she had ever been. We were safer. We didn't have to worry about starvation. We didn't have to wake up next to a man who had frozen to death. We slept in warm beds. We had Shabbat dinner most every Friday. We sometimes even roasted marshmallows in our fireplace.

One day as we were wrapping up a phone conversation

and I was getting ready to meet Jennifer for lunch my mother said, "I called the woman from the Shoah Foundation and they're going to be interviewing me next month."

"So you decided to do it?"

"Yes," she said, and as I left my office and started walking toward the restaurant, I tried to imagine when and how my mother's story would begin.

I should probably mention that most Wednesdays Jennifer and I *didn't* make love, at least not the kind where we ended up taking off our clothes. Most Wednesdays we ate ice cream or talked or did something else that demanded a little less of ourselves, and for some reason, it was satisfying in a way it never was during my Restless Period, when it seemed that more energy went into keeping sexual box scores than into trying to get to know the woman I wanted to make love with. And as I sat at lunch with Jennifer in the Earthen Jar, a wonderful Indian restaurant run by a wonderful Indian woman, I felt like apologizing, because keeping such box scores seemed like such an unfair thing to do to someone in a relationship. It seemed unfair to everyone. I reached across the table and took her hands in mine.

"I think I'm ready," Jennifer said as we were finishing our meal, and by her smile I could tell she was ready for something *big*, but I wasn't sure if it was buying a minivan or completing her graduate work or refinishing our wood floors, which was *really* big when you consider the hassle of having to move the furniture and not being able to live in the house for a few days.

"Ready for what?" I asked, and then it dawned on me what she was ready for, that it wasn't within the domains of automotive retail or graduate education or home improvement; it was within the domain of reproduction. She was ready to have another baby, and I was ready, too. I was so ready that I would have made love on the floor of the Earthen Jar next to the buffet table of succulent vegetarian dishes and chutneys and yogurt dressing, but she suggested we go to my office.

It is one of the advantages of being a psychologist in private practice: you have an office where you can make love with your soulmate. An office that looks kind of like a living room with a sofa and love seat and lamps. Only on that day, my office didn't *feel* like the living room I grew up in. There wasn't that tension in the air, so it was a much better kind of living room for making love, since tension can take the wind out of any two lovers' sails. It can make you want to put up your hands for protection, and most anyone knows that you can't protect yourself and make love at the same time. You have to decide to do one or the other.

As we went up to my office and held each other on the couch I got a sense that we were about to make more than love, that we were about to make *life*. It is hard to describe what the difference is between making love and making life, but I'm sure any couple who has left their diaphragm or birth control pills outside their bedroom door have a sense of the exhilaration that goes along with trying to create a human being, without the benefit of any special equipment or computer programs or consultation, with just their love and their destinies and forces of life rushing through them. And, oh, can love and destiny and forces of life rush through you. It can be like flying. It *was* like flying, the kind of flying that sometimes happens in dreams when you just keep going up and up and the pleasure of weightlessness is wonderfully overwhelming. Only this time I was flying with Jennifer. I wasn't flying alone. We were flying so that our hearts were touching, creating the beginnings of a third heart. This is what lifemaking is like. It is that joint flying where your hearts are touching. That is the best way that I can describe it.

22

PUT YOURSELF

In Your Partner's Shoes

I SOMETIMES WONDER what it'd be like to be a woman, not in the Dennis Rodman sense, wearing silky scarves and high-heel shoes (things that most of the women I know don't even like to wear), but more in the sense that I might better understand Jennifer and the part of me that is like her, the part of me that is maternal.

However, the hard thing about *really* being maternal— or being an actual mother—is that you have to do it all the time. You can't just turn over mothering to the mother, because you're her. It's probably also not easy to have to deal with a man, that is, for those women who are sharing their life with one. That's the part of being a woman I really wouldn't like. Some guy caught up with how well he was or wasn't doing in life. Always wanting to be praised for every little thing he did around the house.

Then there's all this pressure that women seem to be under to be *perfect*—you know, being pretty and bright and patient and friendly and loving and fit, and also having some cooking skills, as well as a clean house in case anyone happens to drop by, and then having to know how to check a child's fever with the back of your hand—and I wouldn't want to have to deal with that. And I wouldn't want to have to control my temper so much of the time either if I were a woman. There is something liberating about being a guy and being able to tell some other guy to fuck himself—like when you take a hard foul on the basketball court—and knowing that minutes later neither of you will think much of it.

I'm also not sure if I'd like sex as much if I were a woman—or if I'd like to have it as frequently. I can see how you'd need to be more in the mood to have sex if you're a woman, the way you need to be in the mood to invite guests to come into your home. I know there are times when my children will stick their fingers in my ears or mouth and I just won't be in the mood for it. I'll say, "Daddy doesn't want anything stuck in his ears right now." Then they'll almost always ask, "Why?" And I'll have to explain to them how it doesn't feel good or how I just want to have my ears to myself at times, knowing all the while how it's impossible for them to appreciate how something that is so much fun for them can be so little fun for me.

Rape would also scare me if I were a woman. I wouldn't like feeling restricted from going out alone at night, and yet I also wouldn't want to have to worry about some psychopath using me for his sadistic outlet. I heard from a woman yesterday that a rape occurs in this country every minute, which adds up to over a half-million rapes a year, and it is hard to believe that isn't seen as being a more urgent problem, that there aren't front-page headlines *every* day reading RAPE EPIDEMIC STILL TERRORIZES THE COUN-TRY or NO ONE HAS FIGURED OUT YET HOW TO STOP RAPE. I mean, at the risk of sounding dogmatic, you can bet there'd be a more urgent response if a half-million white guys in suits were being dragged out of their cars and sodomized each year. That would surely get everyone's attention real quick.

But one thing I'd have to say I would like about being a woman is being pregnant. Few things still seem stranger and more magical to me than the notion that a human being can live inside another human being, that a woman can be a walking ecodome. If I were the producer of a local news telecast, in addition to giving the day's and month's rape update, I'd also show lots of pregnancies and births, maybe a birth every two or three minutes. I'd skip all the endless meteorological minutiae about cloud activity over Iowa (unless the telecast was actually in Iowa) and get right to who was being born that day, who we needed to welcome to the world. I'd also make a point of mentioning all those who died that day, so everyone else could have a chance to say good-bye. And I'd top off each telecast with at least a ten-minute lowdown of the sports news, particularly during basketball season.

One of the reasons it's so important in a relationship to put ourselves in our partner's shoes is that it allows us to have compassion for our partner, which means that we can use this compassion to create a better relationship instead of just feeling resentful about not getting what we want. There is a difference between knowing what we want and need in a relationship and being able to create a relationship where *both* our needs and our partner's needs can be fulfilled; and this difference isn't just about how psychologically insightful we can sound (or are) about ourselves or our partner or how the two of us work together. The difference seems to be more about how much we can feel *for* our partner, how willing we are to take the time to appreciate what it's like to be that person.

This, in turn, might also help us not to take everything our partner does so personally, to understand that when they're tired or cranky it could just be that they're wrestling to get on friendlier terms with themselves—instead of just feeling hurt, which can be an easy thing to feel when we want attention from someone who isn't able to give it to us.

Not only can appreciating what it's like to be our spouse help us to not take everything so personally, it might also help us to be a better friend to them. We might be able to say, "Quit being so hard on yourself" or "Quit thinking that being a mother means you need to enjoy your children every minute." I mean, doesn't it sometimes seem that a piece of the puzzle that is often missing in our relationships is the piece of thinking of how we can help our partner, how we can be a better friend? I know it was missing for me in my Restless Period, and the truth is, sometimes that piece is still missing. I guess it just takes practice—or trust—to not think of yourself first, especially when you're in the throes of parenthood and it seems you have to do so much for your children, from getting them cups of juice, to dressing them, to carrying them when they're tired, week after week after week, until one day your daughter gets her own juice and is able to walk with you all the way to the bakery by herself, and even though she has yet to turn five, it feels that she is practically all grown, that college is just around the corner, and a part of you wishes she'd go back to needing you as much as she once did.

When I mentioned that it takes *trust* to put yourself in your partner's shoes, to not think of yourself first, what I mean by this is that you need to trust that your partner will put you first in the same way, that in this scheme, someone will be thinking of you. In other words, you have to let go of the competitive notion that any one person can win in a relationship, which ultimately is also the truth on a much larger scale of humankind.

I thought of this when one day I saw a homeless woman with a child on the street and it made me question if it was greedy of my wife and me to want a third child when we, humanity, were doing such a piss-poor job of taking care of those we had. Even Nikki, who had yet to turn five, thought it might be a good idea to adopt, "so that way a kid who didn't have a mommy and daddy could then have one." It made rational sense, and yet this whole business of reproduction can be so irrational, can have so much to do with our need to create and be part of a bigger tribe, a tribe consisting of people who look a little like you and act a little like you and give you this comforting feeling of being with kin.

The good thing, though, about being in a relationship, particularly a parenting partnership, is that you can be with someone who is also a little *different* from you, someone who can rise to the occasion in ways and at times that you can't. It is the aspect of single parenthood that I imagine to be indescribably difficult: you have no one to pick you up, no one to facilitate the teeth brushing and baths when you don't have it in you to do it. And I mention teeth brushing and baths because, for whatever reason, all the bedtime chores that take place in my home between the time we march the "opposition" upstairs and the time we actually kiss them good night can feel as uphill a climb as a stroll up San Francisco's Lombard Street. Also, it doesn't help matters that Jennifer feels compelled to stretch out this period with endless stories and rounds of fruit slices and milk, as if we were sending them off on a trip to mainland China instead of just tucking them in for the night.

In our family, Jennifer tends to be the lead parent at bedtime, when my parenting powers are predictably at a low, and I tend to be the lead parent in the morning, when I feel ready to take on any challenge family life can throw our way, while Jennifer is still trying to cope with the difficult transition between her last stage of REM sleep and her morning cup of coffee. I'm not familiar with any research involving "night people" and "morning people," but with most of the couples that I know the woman tends to be the one who likes—or needs—to wake up more slowly (and later), while the guy can pretty much jump out of bed and be ready for action in about the same time that it takes a firefighter to slide down the pole.

The one exception to our parenting arrangement is on bath nights, when both of us are required to be lead parents, when I have to forgo the luxury of meditatively sweeping the kitchen floor by myself or catching the first quarter of a televised basketball game. I sometimes thought that if we had a bigger bathroom it might make the job of bathing our children easier, but I suppose the reality is that if you see a bath as a necessary act of hygiene and your children see it as an opportunity for unbridled recreation then there is the potential for stress even if you have a bathroom the size of a racquetball court.

I was giving Nikki a bath one night while Jennifer was trying to change Alex's diaper, and as he cried and cried in protest, it occurred to me how unreasonable children could be. I mean, here Jennifer was trying to do something that would make *him* more comfortable and he was fighting her as if his life depended on it. Then all of a sudden his crying stopped and an eerie silence filled the house, and within seconds Jennifer was screaming and carrying Alex to me in her arms, and when I looked down at my son he was turning blue and his eyes were rolling back into his head, and I yelled for Jennifer to call 911, while I turned him upside down with my palm against his abdomen and began patting his back, not knowing if he had choked on something, not knowing what had happened, just feeling this overwhelming sense that my boy was about to leave me, that he was about to be taken to wherever Rebecca had been taken to, and it didn't feel as if there was anything I could do besides pat his back and say, "Don't leave, Alex. Don't leave. Please don't leave." And within seconds he began whimpering and life started returning to him, but by that time the ambulance was on its way, and when the medics finally came upstairs and explained how young children can sometimes get themselves so worked up when they're upset that they can hyperventilate and pass out, I thought to myself, "Alex, I will kick your precious ass if you ever do this again."

Then the medics left and we answered all of Nikki's questions about ambulances, breathing, oxygen, 911, the phone system, hypodermic needles, stretchers, medical education, sirens, and the speed limit, and I was finally left once again with the sobering reality of how fragile life is. And in that moment I put myself in my mother's shoes and thought, "Oh, so this is what it's like to be you. This is what it's like to have your heart ripped out of your chest. This is what it's like to lose everything." Because as I held Alex and he was turning blue it did feel that I was about to lose everything, even though he was just one crucial piece of my life. I could feel a part of me dying and turning blue with him and I was quite certain then that if he had died, I would again never be able to trust life and enjoy it in the same way. It was truly my most frightening experience as a parent, my most frightening experience of my entire life, and years later I would still look back on it and shudder, the way you shudder when it occurs to you how the same things that make your life feel so magically full can just as easily make it feel tragically empty.

23

TRUST
Your Destiny

I KNOW it can be hard to trust something you can't control, something that has nothing to do with what you eat or how much money you make or how often you exercise. Because most of us are taught that those who work the hardest, those who really put their noses to the grindstone, get the better life, almost as if we were all entered in a Better Life Tournament that only rewards the top competitors.

I know I used to feel this way for much of my Restless Period, that life was a competition and I was losing. Then a client gave me a copy of the *Tao Te Ching*, a book that I thought everyone stopped reading in the '70s, and I read that "when you realize there is nothing lacking, the whole world belongs to you." This didn't make much sense to me, because it seemed that a lot was lacking in my life, including an intimate connection with my wife and financial security, and yet the message that I figured Lao-tzu was trying to give was that if you accept the present and have faith in the future then your karmic steering wheel will keep you from driving off the more dangerous cliffs.

But while Lao-tzu probably had tragedies of his own, he never had a sister who was killed in a motorcycle accident, and so maybe it was easier for him to write about the universe being as it should be. When someone close to you dies—particularly someone so young—the tendency is more toward wanting to write about the universe seeming kind of fucked-up. Lao-tzu was also into this thing called nonattachment. In addition, he wasn't Jewish, and as we all know, Jews tend to be more into a thing called very intense attachment. They're attached to their families, friends, and favorite restaurants in a way that Taoists probably aren't. And, really, anyone who has a family, anyone who is in love for that matter, always feels there is a tremendous amount at stake in those outcomes that affect the well-being of loved ones.

A minor challenge of trusting your destiny, of having *faith*, is that you run the risk of some people thinking you're not very sophisticated. I know that a number of psychologists, particularly analysts, seem to have a prejudice against the religious beliefs of their clients with strong faith. They might even view their clients' faith as some kind of defense, as some kind of infantile wish to have a parent figure take care of them. This, of course, is all wrong. It is just one example of the science of psychology thinking that life is a subset of *it* rather than the other way around. And I wish I could have taken at least one course in faith as a graduate student, because faith can play a role in the healing of many psychological problems, particularly those involving fear and panic, such as what some of us experience to a greater or lesser extent while flying on an airplane.

When you think about it, a fear-of-flying problem is really a faith problem, since a part of flying comfortably is having faith that the travel gods, or whatever god you believe in, will protect you from crashing into the ocean—and maybe even protect you after you've crashed into the ocean, after you've taken your last breath here on earth and are headed for the other side. Because in order to fly you have to trust that Something will protect you, since it is unlikely you'll be able to do much to protect yourself, even though some control freaks, such as myself, try to envision themselves climbing out of a fiery fuselage and escaping to safety. Wrong. When a plane goes down, we go down with it, and strangely enough, accepting that reality can be more comforting than trying to fight it, trying to control something that isn't within our power to control.

Love is another thing that isn't within our power to control. This doesn't mean that trying to keep our hearts open doesn't help tremendously—it probably helps a lot more than anything you can do for yourself on an airplane—and yet there still are times we must accept that we are passengers in love just as we might be passengers on a flight leaving from Detroit Metro to La Guardia. What makes flights of love unique is that they're never nonstop and the destinations always remain unknown, which might give you some sense of how important trust can be in a loving relationship. I mean, can you imagine what it'd be like to board a flight whose destination you didn't know?

Do you believe that you and your partner are destined to be together? I ask this because it seems that our Restless Periods, or other challenging periods, can be so much harder if we don't have this sense, if we feel that we're with our partner due to coincidence or even bad luck. But just because you feel that you and your partner are destined to be together that might not mean that you're destined to *stay* together. Your destiny might be that you were meant to come together and say good-bye, that your relationship might be just one stop—hopefully not like a bad layover—for each of you in your journeys of love. That's why it's so important to use our intuition, our gut feelings, when it comes to trying to get a sense of the destiny of a relationship. It might be easier initially to take a more passive approach and assume that you and your partner are meant to continue whatever the two of you have started, and yet in the end it's never easy to be living *against* your destiny, as anyone with a basement full of regrets will tell you.

Then there is the reality that while we are living our lives we might never fully know what is best for us. We might just have to go with our best hunches and trust that everything will work itself out in the end. And my experience has been that everything *does* seem to work itself out in the end, including all that I've worried and worried about, such as finding a partner, graduate program, job, house, etc. Maybe the truth is that we eventually do find what we need, even though what we initially thought we needed might not be the same as what we discover we needed down the road. I once heard someone on the radio say—most of my new knowledge does seem to come courtesy of NPR nowadays—that while we might have our own ideas about what is best for us, the universe might have other ideas, and never is this concept illustrated so clearly as when a relationship doesn't work out, and the expected heartache follows, and then years later you find yourself in an even better relationship.

What is hard, though, is to trust your destiny—or at least keep an open mind about it—even when you're going through something terrible. I've never brought up the word *destiny* around my mother for this reason, because I know the last thing she needs is for me, or anyone, to imply that Rebecca was *meant* to die. Not that I necessarily even believe this myself, but I do think she had a sense that she wasn't going to live very long. I remember at the funeral a close friend of hers told Jennifer and me that Rebecca had mentioned that she was planning to write a play about a young woman who leaves New York City for a brief period to find herself in Jamaica. When her friend asked her how the play ended, Rebecca said, "I'm not sure. I just know that it ends in Jamaica, that that's where it all ends."

Rebecca lived her play instead of writing it.

I also make a point of not talking about destiny around couples who are having fertility problems. Jennifer and I have been extremely fortunate in this regard, but we both have friends who have suffered through a roller coaster of expectations and disappointments, involving time and money and doctor's appointments and harsh medications, all of which provide no guarantees. And if you and your partner have fertility problems, it is important to remember: Beautiful people die, beautiful people aren't able to have children. It has nothing to do with what kind of parents you and your partner would be, nor does it have to do with what either of you have done in the past. It isn't a consequence. It isn't a punishment. It just *is*, in the same way that death just is.

When you are fortunate enough to have children, you can come to appreciate that your children have a destiny just as you have a destiny. They have one right off the bat. You see them becoming someone right before your eyes, and it doesn't even seem to be so much a result of your parenting; it seems to be more a result of something within them, a force that pushes them to become who they were meant to become. And you come to appreciate how important it is to respect that force and not try to control it too much.

Destiny facilitation: a new way to look at parenthood.

JENNIFER WAS one day late for her period, which meant that the time had come to head up to the neighborhood drugstore and buy a home pregnancy test, a device that appears no more high-tech at first glance than a toothbrush. I always thought that, considering the importance of what it was measuring, a home pregnancy test might contain a computer chip and run on minute and very expensive batteries. As is often the case nowadays in drugstores, I had to choose between buying the more expensive name-brand one and the less-expensive generic equivalent; and I went with the name-brand model because I didn't want to run the risk of our fetus not feeling as good as other fetuses as a result of its old man trying to save a few bucks.

I took the home pregnancy test up to the cash register and stood in line behind a woman who was purchasing a bottle of calcium supplements, and it occurred to me that you could tell a lot about a person's life by what they purchased at a drugstore. It didn't seem so very long ago that I was in high school buying condoms and Jovan Musk Oil.

I took home the pregnancy test and we read the directions, which were essentially the same as when we were awaiting confirmations from both Nikki's and Alex's souls. The directions were: pee on the applicator stick and wait to see if a matching red dot emerged; a matching red dot meant you were going to have a baby; no matching red dot meant you weren't going to have a baby, at least not right then. It had been a long time since I'd felt so excited, and I wanted to hold Jennifer's hand, not that she really had a free hand available during the procedure. We then left the bathroom and lay down on our bed for five minutes, wondering what fate had in store for us, wondering who we would tell first if we had good news.

We both agreed that we would tell my mother.

Jennifer was too nervous to go check the test, and so I went into our bathroom, as if I was heading into the most magical of caves, and what I found was more precious than any jewel or gem; it was the red dot, the dot of life, the dot of creation. And I screamed out to Jennifer that we were going to have a baby, that we were going to have another child, and in that moment it truly did seem that nothing was lacking and the whole world belonged to us,

and to my mother and her family as well, and to all the
people who had once been a part of her family, the people
whom I never had a chance to meet, the ones whom I had
seen only one or two times in my dreams.

WE WAITED until the weekend to share the news with my
mother, because we were all planning on coming in for her
Shoah interview. She wanted to be able to introduce us at
the end of the interview, after she'd had a chance to tell
her life's story. I spoke with her briefly on the phone the
night before and she let me know how scared she was to
talk about her war experiences, experiences that she had
never really talked about with anyone, experiences that she
hadn't thought about in years. "I'm afraid I might start
crying," she said, and I tried to assure her that that should
be the least of her concerns, that this was an interview
where it was okay to cry, where it was expected she'd cry,
as compared to a job interview where she was expected to
perform.

It was strange being in her backyard the next day, as
she sat inside her living room being interviewed by the
Shoah staff. It was strange in the sense that I imagined
how strange it must be for her, living in the suburbs in a
nice house some forty years after she and so many others
had emerged from their collective nightmare. Did it feel
unreal for her? Did she ever walk down the aisles of a
supermarket and look around at all the food and think, "I
came so close to starving to death"? Did she ever walk into

her warm house and recall the winter she and her family fled Warsaw after the Nazi invasion?

It was also strange that my daughter and son were in her backyard, living the childhood that she never had a chance to live. They were kicking a soccer ball. They were sitting on the grass with bowls of pretzels and sippy cups of lemonade. They were enjoying a childhood without destruction, a childhood without death. It was still hard to imagine that she was only seven when it all began. Seven is when most kids are finishing up first grade. They are getting up the nerve to sleep over at their friends' houses. They are going to the latest Disney movie with their grandparents. They are not fearing annihilation. Go to a school playground and watch some seven-year-olds if you don't believe me. I promise that you won't see any of them questioning their survival. I promise they'll all seem immortal to you, every last one of them.

And before we were called inside the house to join my mother, I thought how impossible it must be for her to trust her destiny after all she's been through. It would be understandable if she couldn't trust anything, and yet remarkably she could trust, only she did it while simultaneously preparing for "rainy days." I could remember her using this expression when I was a boy, suggesting that I might want to "save my snow shoveling money for a rainy day." But years later, as a man, I couldn't help but wonder what there was about rain to fear. Rain didn't hurt us. It didn't take away anything that was precious. In fact, it was what made so many precious things grow.

Then we went inside and sat on the couch with my mother and it was clear she *had* been crying, but it was also clear that she knew it was okay, that she felt safe. And being on the couch with her husband, son, daughter-in-law, and grandchildren seemed to make her feel more safe. She looked so happy and relieved to have us by her side, there for her at the end of her journey. She introduced us to the camera, and the interviewer welcomed any of us to say what we wanted, and Nikki went on to talk about how "Grandma had been in a war when she was a girl and that wars were bad"; and I briefly mentioned how proud I was of my mother and how much I loved her; and then there was silence and in that silence I felt Rebecca's presence, I felt her love, just as I would have if she had walked into the room. I even moved down on the couch and made a space for her. I made a space right between my mother and me.

24

PICK UP
After Yourself

IT IS NATURAL for us to want to be cared for by another person, to want to be cared for by our partner, but relationships seem to work much better when the way we want to be cared for is compatible with the way our partner wants to care for us. And most people don't want to care for someone by cleaning up their messes, especially if that someone is a man in his thirties or forties. It is a little different if that someone is a two-year-old child, and even then there isn't much that's touching about a mess; it is still a mess.

So if you're a man who is looking for ways to rejuvenate your love life, I have some simple advice: Before you hire a personal trainer and begin a weight training program, before you invest in Italian clothing or send your partner roses, you might want to try picking your socks up off the floor. You'd be surprised what an effective aphrodisiac consideration is. The reason it's so underrated is that I don't think anyone has figured out a way to make money off it. It's not like other aspects of sex appeal where the average consumer is made to feel that if she doesn't wear the right antiperspirant or the right underwear no one will want to be in an intimate relationship with her for the rest of her life.

But I think with the right creative touch someone could put together an erotic magazine for women that is based on consideration. The magazine could show pictures of a handsome man sweeping up a kitchen floor or vacuuming a carpet with his tired partner resting her feet in the background, and underneath the picture could be a caption like "I think it's only natural to want to make life easier for someone you care about." I could be wrong, but I think a magazine like this would catch on quickly, especially with mothers of young children.

It seems that one of the reasons being considerate can be so challenging for both men and women is that it forces us to take responsibility for the quality of our relationships, something that most of us aren't inclined to do when we're feeling exhausted or discouraged or anxious or blue. When we're feeling any of the above things, we're much more inclined to have our partner do everything for us, which most partners are willing to do, just as long as the arrangement is reciprocal. The problems occur when we want to be babied exclusively, when we won't take turns and assume the role of the mom or dad. That is when the arrangement ceases to be fun, when our partner begins thinking of a way to put us up for adoption.

Does all this business about being a baby or a mom or dad in an adult relationship sound strange? I don't think it has to be strange, at least not *bad* strange. Because being in an intimate relationship puts all of us in touch with younger sides of ourselves, and if we can't figure out a way for this younger side to be expressed and cared for, we will inevitably end up feeling like a displaced orphan. What is worse is that we might also end up feeling like a bitter orphan, and the sad reality is that no one wants to take care of someone who is bitter. It is what's so dangerous about bitterness: no one wants to take care of you, you have to figure out a way to take care of yourself. And since most bitter people are incapable of taking care of themselves, they just end up feeling more bitter, which makes the possibility of them being loved even more remote.

And when I say that being in an intimate relationship puts us in touch with a younger part of ourselves, I'm not talking about middle school or high school younger; I'm talking about pre-orgasm, pre-Levi's, just-wanting-to-be-held younger. Because there really is no way to get around feeling this young in a relationship. In part, it's all the touching and holding that does it, the sensation of our skin against the skin of our loving partner; because that sensation is so powerful it can awaken the most dormant need for physical closeness, along with memories of when this physical closeness might not have been available to us to the extent that we needed it.

I think that was a part of what happened to me in my Restless Period: a dormant need for physical closeness was awakened and I didn't quite know how to handle it. Dormant needs for physical closeness are never easy to handle. They can be overwhelmingly scary because of how helpless and clingy they make us feel. I know there was one morning when I woke up, looked in the mirror, and said, "I am the Neediest Person on the Planet." This was after I had a dream of being a young child caught alone in a snowstorm. I didn't remember much about the dream, but I didn't have any food and what scared me most was that I could just keep walking and walking without ever finding anyone. It was the possibility of never finding anyone that scared me more than the cold. I had on a warm coat and thick mittens and the cold really didn't bother me.

Have you ever woken up (or gone to bed) feeling like you were the Neediest Person on the Planet? I found that I began feeling much better once I confessed that this was how I felt, once I finally got up the nerve to come out of the closet. Because what is worse than admitting to yourself you feel like the Neediest Person on the Planet is actually feeling this way and pretending that you don't. That is when you're most at risk for leaving your socks on the floor and being needy in a way that pushes your partner away. That is when you're most at risk for being a demanding and sullen prick.

In contrast, if you're able to accept your neediness, you might find that your needs draw your partner closer to you, which is always a neat thing for needs to do. Actually, that is what needs are *designed* to do. Children are wired to need their parents and parents are wired to meet the needs of their children. You see how smoothly this arrangement works in nature (i.e., nature shows) where little lion cubs attach themselves to their mothers, and through their attachment, manage to get *everything* they need. Things aren't quite so simple with humans. For one, humans have a whole assortment of emotional needs that are probably harder to fulfill than a lion cub's need for zebra or yak meat; and also human mothers, human parents, are faced with more competing demands than the typical lioness. It also doesn't help that human mothers aren't a part of a pride the way lions are, having a network of adult females to help care for the cubs, the males needed only for reproductive purposes and to ward off an occasional predator.

Another thing different about humans is that when they don't get their emotional needs met they tend to be angry with themselves for needing too much rather than being angry with their caretaker or parent for giving too little. This isn't something a lion would do. Lions always accept their needs at face value and never try to lessen or short-circuit them, even in the worst dry season, so to speak. In fact, it is in the dry season, when the odds of their needs being met is reduced, that the lions become even more loyal to their desires, to the point that they will risk their lives and go after a cape buffalo, an animal whose sharp horns and immense power make it a lethal puncturing machine.

While a part of being human might be that we never get *everything* we need as children, and while some of us *do* get much less than others, it still doesn't mean we have a right to demand that our partners make up for a time when our parents might have dropped the ball. In other words, if you try and make your partner pay for the sins of your parents you will invite another "dry season" into your life that will leave your soul parched with the worst déjà vu; because no one wants to pay for anyone else's sins. I should say here that I really don't believe that anything my mother or father did to me was a sin. It was more just a sequel to their own childhoods, a sequel that by all accounts was much gentler and kinder.

However, if you're a man who is hoping to recoup in your marriage some of the nurturing that might have been absent in your childhood, I should remind you that the best time to do this isn't when your partner is in the first trimester of her pregnancy. Women in their first trimester tend not to be all that reliable as active nurturers. They are probably a lot like malaria patients, sleeping whenever they get a chance, using the words *rest* and *tired* every two or three sentences. One of Jennifer's mothering magazines went so far as to advise that whenever a pregnant woman is faced with a choice between sleep and anything else, she should always choose sleep. A fathering magazine might suggest a different choice on occasion.

For the most part, I didn't mind helping out more around the house while Jennifer was pregnant. I figured it was the least I could do, since she was the one who was carrying our child and would eventually give birth to it. For the time being, we still referred to our baby as "it," having yet to receive any strong omens or medical hunches about the sex of our child. My first inclination was to think we were going to have a girl, since our family had just lost a girl—a twenty-eight-year-old girl—and it was natural to think that's what we were going to get back. The bottom line, though, was that we just wanted our child to be born healthy, and that wasn't something we just said for the sake of reproductive diplomacy, that really was the bottom line.

I enjoy cooking much more than cleaning, which is probably true of most men who are drawn to the glory of preparing a tasty meal, especially a tasty meal for his children and pregnant wife. In contrast, I find less glory in housecleaning, a facet of domestic life that only receives attention when it is neglected. A clean house basically goes unnoticed, and that was something I came to appreciate more during Jennifer's first trimester, how thankless a job it was to keep cleaning up after other people, sweeping the same floors, clearing the same table, washing the same dishes. It doesn't matter how much you love the people who are creating all the mess; it is still a thankless job.

Pregnant women also tend to be rather critical of their environment, and there is nothing worse than working hard to clean a house, only to have someone afterward point out all the things that you failed to clean. It was in moments like these that I thought there should be some kind of spa or halfway house for pregnant women, a place that was immaculately clean and offered unlimited meal options, along with a courier service for off-hour cravings. But I knew what Jennifer was going through was just a stage, and when you know something's just a stage, it is that much easier to cope with it. I think that's what was so tough with all the stuff we went through during our most difficult times: neither of us knew when it would stop, or even *if* it would stop.

I was sweeping out behind our dresser one evening—

doing "deep cleaning" as Jennifer referred to it—when I came across a photograph that my brother, Ezra, must have sent me a few years back. I knew it must have come from him, because it was a photograph of me as a young boy, and he was the one who managed to end up with most of these photographs after the divorce, when he and my father pretty much divided them up without any protest from my mother, Rebecca, or myself.

And when I looked at this picture of me sitting on the swing in the backyard of the house where I was born, our house in Woodlawn, I thought of something that I hadn't thought about in years: how I used to rock myself to sleep every night. I probably did it up until I was about twelve years old, and while my mother thought this was a "resourceful" strategy on my part, I didn't feel resourceful; I didn't feel much of anything. It was just something I did to comfort myself, something I had done for as long as I could remember. But as I got older I knew it was something I'd have to stop, because I was starting to sleep over at friends' houses more, and that wasn't something they did. It was only something I did.

Why did I recall this some twenty years later when I was picking up an old photograph and several stray socks off the floor? I didn't know. I just had a sense that if I could lie down next to Jennifer and rest my cheek against her warm body I would feel better, that it would comfort that thing inside me that used to be comforted by rocking myself to sleep at night, and so that's what I did. I took the photograph into bed with me, too, as if I were afraid to leave the younger me alone for too long. For a second,

I thought I might even fall asleep, but I didn't. I just lay quietly and breathed in Jennifer's sweet, maternal scent; then a while later, when I was feeling lighter about things, I brought the photograph up to her breast and she pretended to nurse this younger image of me. It wasn't something she minded doing. We both laughed as a drop of breast milk fell on the photograph, just laughed and laughed the way you do when a joke or irony suddenly provides you with a tremendous sense of relief.

25

HUNT FOR GOOD
Childhood Memories

I REALIZE this might involve sorting through a lot of debris, but I think in the long run it is worth it. Even in the short run it can be meaningful to recall an afternoon spent apple picking or a doubleheader down at the ballpark, to recall something that was simple and good. And the good memories do seem so simple, don't they? They usually just involve fun and togetherness and calm and wonder. I suppose they involve everything that bad memories don't.

One thing about bad memories is that they can be the worst of bullies. They'll push down a good memory without thinking twice about it, and when that good memory tries to get up, they won't hesitate to stomp on it. Bad memories are like teenagers in that everything has to be black and white to them, and yet as we get older we realize that everything *isn't* black and white, especially love.

As I look back on our family, it seems that our problems intensified when my father was laid off from his job at General Electric after working there for nearly fifteen years. We were living in Cincinnati at the time, where I

was born, and where Rebecca was also born. Ezra was born
in Israel. That is where my parents met, my mother having
gone to Israel after the war like many other European Jews,
and my father having sailed a ship from Cuba to France to
Haifa to help begin what would become Israel's navy. I
mention this to illustrate that my father was an *idealistic*
man, and to mark how something happened to his idealism
the day he was laid off from General Electric a few weeks
prior to becoming eligible for his pension. This happened
when I was in sixth grade, and he was no longer the same
man after his last day at GE. He changed in the way that
soldiers change after they go to war and it is no longer
possible to believe in life as something that will take care
of them and keep them safe. In fact, the same dazed and
bitter expression on my father's face that night was similar
to the expressions on the faces of the patients at the VA
hospital, where I would work as an intern seventeen years
later. Only this was my father and not a patient. He was
there in the den when I went to sleep and still there when
I woke up in the morning, in the same olive-green vinyl
recliner. I think my father often went days without sleeping
during that time. I knew instinctively to leave him alone,
knew that he wasn't going to be up for tossing a football
around in the street or taking us for a swim at the Jewish
Community Center pool. There were a number of years
when he did do these things with my brother and me, as
the more recreational parent. He took us to Reds games at
Crosley Field where we saw Frank Robinson (before he was
traded to the Orioles) and Pete Rose and Johnny Bench
and Tony Perez. Rebecca came along six years after me,

and so she missed out on most of the years when my father was a more idealistic man; those years were a smaller percentage of her life. It can matter a lot when you come on the scene in your family. You appreciate this more as a parent, when you're aware of how your inner struggles coincide with your child's development. My father was laid off from his job at GE when Rebecca was six years old, an age when all of us seem to get a little better at holding on to our memories.

It's never easy to hunt for memories, or to hunt for anything of value for that matter, and yet I feel an obligation to offer something in the way of guidance. If I'm going to suggest you try something, I should at least be able to help with directions. Of course, there are psychologists who don't believe in offering much in the way of directions or explanations. Some psychologists don't even believe in talking all that much. They just wait defiantly in silence for their clients to open up about themselves, and as you can imagine, it's nearly impossible to open up about yourself to someone who is waiting defiantly in silence. The number one complaint I hear from clients about their former therapists: They just sat there without saying anything. And, unfortunately, a number of these clients left with the feeling that their therapist didn't find them all that interesting.

Sometimes memories leave us for the same reason that clients leave their therapists—because they don't feel we're interested—and so we need to take the necessary steps to prove that we're *really* interested in having them back, that we're waiting with open arms for their return. These steps can include looking through old photographs or talking with relatives or visiting the neighborhood where you grew up; or it can even include taking a quiet break from your daily routine and trying to harvest as many possible images from your earlier life, images of the house you grew up in, the actual rooms, the smell of the basement, your bike in the garage, your seat at the dinner table, the posters on your bedroom wall.

Do you ever take a quiet break from your daily routine? I found that during my Restless Period I couldn't, that all I could do was make lists in my head and then work each day like a bee, trying to check off each item on my list, a process that yielded little in the way of honey, a process that actually only yielded more lists. And I promise you won't remember much of anything important when you're in a list-making mode, because in order to remember we need to feel, and we can't really feel when we're making lists. Maybe that's why most of us make lists. But I found that I grew tired of feeling numb, and so I made a list of why I made lists. It included the following: (1) I was afraid I'd feel lonely if I stopped making them; (2) I was afraid I'd fail in some way.

One of the reasons it can be so valuable to hunt for good childhood memories is that we might discover something that can be of help to us in our adult lives. We might have lost something back there that we need in order to be on friendlier terms with ourselves, something like the ability to trust or the ability to dream or the ability to play. At some point in my Restless Period it occurred to me that I had lost the ability to look forward to things, to get ex-

cited about the possibilities of the unknown; and I say I
lost this ability, because I knew at one point I had it. I
could remember being a boy who could barely contain his
excitement before recess and football games and sleepov-
ers. What happened to this boy? How could I make him
feel welcome enough to return to my life?

I decided to take a trip to Cincinnati to find out.

Before I tell you about the memory trek I took, I should
say that this kind of trek is best taken at a time in your
life when you feel receptive to change. Not just receptive
to it, but hungry for it. Even starved. Otherwise, it will just
feel like you're sightseeing. When you see your old school
or your old neighborhood and think, "Oh, how nice,
they've painted my house a different color," you're only
feeling nostalgia, and the kind of trek that I'm recom-
mending is about more than nostalgia. It is about feeling
countless emotions at once. Everything from adventure to
terror to shame to joy to love to challenge to despair. A
symphony of feeling inside your chest. That is your goal,
and although feeling such a symphony might be a lofty one,
you want to strive to attain it. You don't want to come home
with a simple conclusion that your childhood was either
"good" or "bad," because then you'll end up thinking in
these dichotomous terms as an adult, and you won't really
see your life. You won't grasp how a life can be both good
and bad at the same time—or how it can go from good
to bad, or from bad to good, which is something that all
lives do.

In a perfect world, I would have asked Jennifer to come
with me on this trek, but our imperfect world didn't in-

clude anyone who could take care of our children, so that wasn't an option. It included two sets of grandparents, both of whom lived nearby and loved our children to pieces, but who were not the stereotypical pie-baking kind of grandparents who could take care of a whole brood of kids for weeks at a stretch.

I thought of asking Ezra to join me, but he was more of an emotional wild card, and I wasn't really sure if that's what I wanted or needed. It was a lot easier to ask my friend Bennett, whom I didn't get to see as much now that I was a parent, and who was always up for a road trip. We decided to make it a day excursion, leaving at seven in the morning and getting back before it was dark, so I could be there to say good night to Nikki and Alex. As a parent, I was way at the homebody end of the spectrum, having only been away from our kids one night in a four-year stretch; that was the weekend my mother and I had gone to New York to clear out Rebecca's apartment.

Before my trip Ezra confirmed my suspicions about his suitability as a trek partner when he said, "I wouldn't want to go back to Cincinnati, because I'd be afraid I'd remember the *wrong* things." But I tried to assure myself there were no wrong things to remember as Bennett and I got in the car and headed toward my hometown. It was a beautiful spring day, and we both wore our new sunglasses, which is always a fun thing to buy for yourself before a road trip. We stopped at a highway rest stop that had a '50s-style cafeteria with steaming trays of macaroni and franks and beans, and I thought of something my father had once said to me as a boy when we'd stopped in such a place. We were ordering lunch, and I was very hungry, and after I told him what I wanted to order, he looked at me and said, "Your eyes are too big for your stomach." At the time, I wasn't sure if this meant that my stomach was too small or my eyes were too big, but I knew that my father was displeased with me for wanting so much.

Cincinnati felt surprisingly familiar, even though I hadn't been back there in twenty-five years. I knew all the streets without having to use a map. The first place I visited was the Jewish Community Center, which was kind of a home away from home for me, a place where I went to day camp and played organized football and basketball. This was during the mid and late '60s when Cincinnati still had a professional basketball team—the Royals—who used to practice at the JCC gymnasium, and it was always a thrill to sit along the sidelines and watch the likes of Tiny Archibald, Norm Van Lier, Jumping Johnny Green, and Sam Lacey. I had all their autographs and was free to go in and out of their locker room after practice when they were showering and getting dressed.

There was still a trophy case in the hallway outside the gymnasium and it was a thrill to see my name engraved in the football team's Most Valuable Player trophy, right beneath the names of my older neighbors, two brothers whom I looked up to and tried to emulate. I looked at "Dan Saferstein—1970" and recalled how proud I felt when our coach announced my name at our banquet as our team's "most valuable player." I was only eleven at the time, and that trophy must have been no more than a foot tall, but the specialness I felt when our coach patted me on the back and said "You earned this" wasn't something I would feel with the same intensity for the next twenty-seven years, not until my agent and editor called and expressed interest in this book.

But I could feel the specialness start to slip away as I left the JCC and headed toward my old house, and I didn't know what to do to hold on to it, which I assumed was a problem I had had way back then. We passed what used to be Longview State Mental Hospital and I recalled how eerie a place this used to seem to me, how we would hear stories of patients who were tied up and forced to take ice-cold baths, which didn't seem like something that would make a crazy person less crazy. I began to feel nervous the closer we got to my street, the closer we got to my house, and I could sense a powerful loneliness about to overtake me, and I knew there wasn't anything I could do but be still and let it rush through me, which it did, bringing tears to my eyes, along with the realization of how much I used to hate being alone as a child, how it could feel so terrifying, how I'd have to fight off the fears of someone or something *getting* me.

And it was unclear how this boy who hated to be alone grew up to be a man who forced himself to be alone, who almost needed to prove that this was something he was capable of doing. It seemed it would have made so much more sense to be alone less, since I now had the option to be alone less, which wasn't really an option I had as a child. My life had changed, had become easier in many respects, and yet I was still living as if it hadn't, still living as if specialness was something you had to fight for on a football field or a basketball court or even in a bedroom.

Then when I came to my house I was surprised by how beautiful it looked. I was certain it'd be run down, if not completely leveled to the ground, and yet someone had cared for it and made it beautiful, much more beautiful than it was when we were living there. The lawn was a rich green and the flower beds were full of different-colored tulips, and I looked around and thought it had to be the most beautiful house in the neighborhood. It surely wasn't a house that the owners felt ashamed of living in. You could tell that by how well they had taken care of it, how they'd made sure no part of the exterior was neglected, not even the roof or gutters. I rang the doorbell to ask if I could visit the backyard, but they weren't home, and so I decided just to go there, figuring I'd just look around for a few seconds and leave; but I ended up staying longer, thinking about a time when I was five or six when I nearly set our neighbor's yard on fire, not because I intended to do them harm, but more because I was curious about matches and how fire spread. It wasn't something I had thought about in years, and I wasn't really sure why I was thinking about it then. I wondered if it had something to do with the image of fire burning something down so that something else can grow in its place. I know that conservationists sometimes intentionally set prairie fires for this reason. I have seen them do this, seen the charred earth and the wisps of smoke rising up from the ground. Then after a certain period of time flowers grow. They seem to come from nowhere. I'm not sure how it happens.

26

TAKE

A Vacation

IT DOESN'T HAVE TO BE somewhere exotic. There is probably little correlation between how much money we spend on our vacations and how much fun we have. Most any campground will support this theory, and if you happen to go to one, you'll find people relaxing and enjoying a slower rhythm, enjoying a life without lists. It is one of the joys of vacationing, that you don't have to do anything you don't want to do, unless you happen to go on one of those *demanding* vacations, the kind where you try to see as much as possible in the least amount of time. And while I've never been on such a vacation (i.e., the four countries in ten days tour), my sense is that they are geared more for people who want the pace of their vacation to be similar to the pace of their work, for people who have a low still-ness tolerance.

It is possible, though, to increase our stillness toler-ance, and I mention this because I think the reason we postpone vacations has less to do with the cost of them and more to do with a fear of stillness. Not that this is what we talk about when we decide not to go anywhere; instead, we itemize out loud the cost of airfare, lodging, food, etc.—probably because we think others would look down on us if we confessed how terrified we were of going to a strange place and not doing what we normally do each day, not having the same foods and the same schedule and same whirl of deals and contracts. It can even be an adjustment using a different bathroom.

For people who are overwhelmed by the thought of all this change, there is always the option of taking a vacation without going anywhere, meaning you can take a week off work and just do stuff around the house. But you have to do stuff that is different from what you normally do or else it won't be a vacation; it'll just be your regular life. Also, if you're going to really pursue a home-based vacation some of what you do has to smack of indulgence. You can't just take the time to clean out your basement or lay sod in the backyard, unless you happen to be the rare person who derives intense pleasure from basement cleaning or sod laying. However, it is more often the case that people derive intense pleasure from the sense that something is taking care of them rather than they are taking care of something. That is why the activities on cruises tend not to feature such things as toilet unclogging, garbage disposal fixing, floor waxing, typing, or oil filter changing.

As for the challenge of increasing our tolerance for stillness, a good way to approach this task is to start with a comfortable amount of stillness and then gradually increase it as we become more confident. For the most part, this is a good way to increase our tolerance for *anything*, including togetherness, which definitely comes into play during vacations. That is probably another reason that some of us don't take vacations—too much togetherness. Or maybe it's our fear about how the togetherness will restrict us, since we probably wouldn't fear it if we thought it could only add to our enjoyment possibilities. I mean, what's the point of fearing something that's going to make our experience more enjoyable?

But many men have the prejudice that togetherness with women will be restrictive, and thus will cease to be enjoyable after a while. They don't have this same prejudice about togetherness with men. Togetherness with men is even romanticized by our society. You see it all the time in beer commercials: men having the time of their lives when they're together with other men. Laughing. Fishing. Feeling free. Then doing whatever they can to make sure they can have more of this togetherness. Telling outrageous lies to wives or girlfriends so they can sneak off with their buddies and enjoy cold beer.

The implication of all this seems to be that women are weak and clingy, and that's why it's no fun to be with them; because they demand so much; because they don't know how to be alone; because they can't do more for them- selves. This creates an image of women as a burden, even a financial burden. I can think of one commercial where the wives and girlfriends are heading off to spend the beer-drinking man's money. Money that could otherwise be spent on cold beer. Or if they're not doing that they're just standing around in the kitchen looking displaced, waiting for a pretzel bowl that needs to be refilled. It seems they seldom have real lives.

However, one vacation reality is that if you take young children along it makes the experience all the more challenging. As demanding as parenting can be at home, it can be even more so when the kids are away from the familiarity of their routines. Children who normally nap during the day might never nap while on vacation, or might nap only a fraction of the time, which means that for at least a couple of hours during the afternoon you will fantasize about foster care or the Perfect Relative who could have taken care of them. While all of this might not sound like much of a pitch for the family vacation, most families manage to take them and to come back home with at least a few good memories of their time together.

Some of us also have some bad memories of family vacations. The bad one I can recall was the last vacation our family ever took, when I was about twelve years old. This was after my father was laid off from General Electric, after his idealism had started to go down the drain. He got a new job in Michigan at Conrad Research, a facility that manufactured the steering mechanism for missiles. This was what my father did for five years until he was laid off again: design missile steering wheels. He was given two weeks of vacation a year, and my parents decided that we would use one of the weeks to visit friends of ours in Schenectady, a ten-hour car drive from Detroit.

I mention how long the car drive was because I don't remember anything about the vacation itself; all I remember was my father trying to pass car after car and my mother screaming and Rebecca crying and Ezra looking as if he'd left his soul at a rest stop some hundred miles back. It was like a horror movie that kept replaying itself every half hour or so, and in retrospect, I can't help but wonder if my father was acting out some wish to kill himself, and to kill us in the process. What made everything feel even more insane was that he would break out laughing in spite of how terrified we all were, chuckling to himself how the really good drivers like himself could afford to take *chances* that other drivers couldn't. And I remember thinking, at age twelve, that if I had a bat, I would have swung it with all my might against the back of his head.

In addition to some of the bad vacation associations I had from my childhood, it didn't help that Rebecca died while she was on vacation. That didn't exactly make me want to get out and see the world. In fact, it made me appreciate people who were afraid to leave their houses, people who were convinced that the best way to keep safe was to control your environment and routine so carefully that each day was almost identical to the next, proving to yourself that the future was no more dangerous than the past.

But I didn't want to teach our children to fear life, or to fear life myself, and so we accepted an invitation from our friends, Rick and Madeline, to come visit them in the Berkshires, a resort area where people went all the time without dying. And there didn't seem to be anything dangerous about the Berkshires when we finally arrived. The mountains were short. The trees were perfectly green. The lakes were beautiful. One of the neighbors even had llamas. It was definitely a place where you didn't have to feel afraid, and after a day of relaxation, I could feel what apprehension I had leaving me. Rick and I even took Nikki and Alex for a boat ride, which felt a little more dangerous than petting llamas, but not scary dangerous; it was more exciting, especially for the children. They both sat on my lap as Rick drove the boat, and I could tell how magnificent the world seemed to them at that moment as we flew across the water.

I also enjoyed Rick's company more than I ever had. He seemed more playful and receptive than I remembered him being, and naturally I was curious about what had caused this change in him, since it was a change I was interested in making in myself. It seemed that you couldn't go wrong with the playfulness and receptivity combination, and it not only was something that I noticed and appreciated, but Nikki noticed it as well. She played with Rick in the water and let him pick her up, which she wouldn't do with just anyone, which she wouldn't even do with my own brother.

Jennifer took lots of pictures as we were saying goodbye, and while I often give her a hard time about having to photograph every moment, and then ordering "doubles" of that moment, it was always nice to be able to look back and remember how we were feeling when a picture was taken. The pictures of our children were especially meaningful to me, not so much right when they were taken, but months and years later when they served as markers for their growth and the passage of time.

We were actually sitting at our kitchen table about a week after our vacation and looking at pictures of Rick and Madeline when the phone rang; it rang in such a way that I knew we were about to receive bad news. And this might sound kind of crazy that a telephone could ring in such a way as to hint of tragedy, but it did; I swear it did. And as I saw Jennifer's face go white and heard Madeline weeping on the other end I could feel everything come undone again, the way it had come undone after Rebecca died, and at first it didn't seem possible that I could be with Rick on a boat one week and the next week he could die of an aneurysm, not when he was only thirty-three, not when he seemed so alive when he was playing with Nikki in the water. It just didn't seem possible, and it didn't seem fair, and I couldn't help but think: God, what the fuck are you doing? Have you lost your mind? Is the death function on your computer not working? Because you've really screwed up twice. You've taken people who had their whole lives ahead of them and that's not what you're supposed to be doing. That's not godly. What I mean is that you're ripping people's hearts out each time you do something like this. There are ramifications, God. Do you hear me? Everyone's life is connected to every other life. So it's not like you're just taking people to be with *you*. You're taking them away from someone. You took Rick away from Madeline. They were going to have children. What was your point? I just want some simple answers. I want to know why you took Rebecca and why you took Rick. Is that too much to ask for someone who is struggling to have faith in you? I'd like to think that it isn't, that you're a god that can withstand

and love any question, and if this truly is the case, I have one more question for you, God: What next? Who are you going to take next? My wife? One of my children? Because if you're lonely, God, if what you need is company, come and take me. Don't take anyone I love. Just come for me, God. You know where I am.

27

LET SADNESS
Visit You

OUR VISITS with Sadness don't necessarily have to be
that long. Sometimes this seems to be what we fear most
about Sadness, that she will come, unpack her bags, and
never want to leave. Then we will be stuck with Sadness as
a permanent companion. She will be with us when we want
to play golf. She will be with us when we need to go to
work. And we won't quite know how to introduce her, especially to those friends and colleagues who haven't ap-
peared to have hung out much with Sadness, the myriad of
Happy People who seem to hop effortlessly from their jobs
to the gym to their personal lives without any surprise visits from Sadness or her cousins Hurt and Anger.

The Happy People can be scary. We're afraid they'll look
down on us and ask, "Who's that you've got with you?"
And then we'll have to say, "It's Sadness. That's who's with
me." But I have a little secret to tell: The Happy People
know Sadness better than you think. They know her cousins as well. I can tell you this because for the longest time
others looked at me as a Happy Person. They looked at me

this way because I had a wonderful wife and because I excelled in sports and because I was a psychologist, which should have been a clue that this wasn't the case, since a truly Happy Person probably wouldn't choose to become a psychologist. The time a psychologist spends face-to-face with struggle wouldn't appeal to a Happy Person, and yet there *does* seem to be something about struggle—the coming together of Sadness, Hurt, Anger, Action, etc.—that appeals to most everyone. The folks in Hollywood know this. That is why they include struggle in so many of their films.

Does it seem odd to you that I refer to sadness as a *she*? I do this because there can be something soft about sadness, and in my lifetime I have come to associate softness with the feminine. That is one of the reasons women have meant so much to me—because of the softness they have brought to my life, because of the softness they have let me borrow from them. For the longest time, it wasn't something I could manufacture on my own, and getting it from other men never seemed like a good idea. Men just had a different way about them. They were too much like I was. They always had to be *doing* something, and even when they weren't doing something, they seemed to be *thinking* about what they were going to do next.

If you're a man who is interested in manufacturing his own softness, you might need to become more like a woman. Before you run out of the room and do your obligatory fifty to seventy-five push-ups, please listen closely: this doesn't mean you have to change your wardrobe or stop watching ESPN or venture into the confusing and expensive world of hair-care products. It just means that you might need to relate to your emotions and share them more as women do, because the essence of female softness is rooted in how women relate to their emotional lives. It's not rooted in cleavage or anything like that.

I realize that I have been talking about sadness and softness in the same breath, and this is because there is an intricate relationship between sadness and softness. You can't be soft unless you can be sad and you can't be sad unless you can be soft. Let me explain: What happens to people who try to insulate themselves from sadness is that they also end up insulating themselves from *every* feeling—with the possible exception of anger—and this leaves them as hard and inflexible as concrete. In other words, you can't repress emotions à la carte; when you repress one, you repress them all.

Then there's the challenge of figuring out what the more meaningful things are for us to feel sad about, the things that are closer to our hearts. Often we make the mistake of feeling sad about our imperfections, which really is approaching the task of sadness all wrong. It is making sadness out to be about beauty pageant results, and there is really more to sadness than body fat or the whiteness of our teeth. I should probably backtrack for a second and say that the most meaningful sadness isn't something we have to figure out; it comes to us, comes to us in the same way that love comes to us. We could be sitting at our desk or driving down the road and all of a sudden it appears by our side, wanting to be with us. That is sometimes all sadness wants: just to be with us. Not to be fixed. Not to be explained. Children can be like this. They'll bump their heads or scrape their knees and come in our laps, knowing that there's nothing we can do to take their pain away, that all we can do is be with their pain.

After Rick died, I wasn't quite sure how sad to be around our children. I didn't want to burden them with my sadness, and yet I also didn't want them to learn that sadness was something that had to be kept a secret, that it was something to fear; because then they would be afraid of their own sadness and do all they could to keep it a secret. And I soon discovered there was nothing really frightening to them about sadness. They seemed quite comfortable with it. Nikki asked a lot of questions about aneurysms. She wanted to know if you could feel one that was in your head. She wanted to know if Rick knew ahead of time that he was going to die. I told her that he didn't.

"Do Rick and Madeline have any children?" Nikki asked, as I was tucking her into bed.

"No, honey. Why do you ask?"

"Because that would mean they wouldn't have a daddy," she said, and as I kissed her good night and left her room I felt determined to keep a couple steps ahead of death for many years to come. God would have to find someone else to be with him if he felt lonely. He would have to join a book discussion group. He would have to start hanging out in cafés. Because I had two young children and a third on the way, and in my mind, that meant that I should be exempt from death the way medical students were once exempt from the military draft.

Of course, I knew there were no exemptions when it came to mortality, and Rick's death served to remind me

of this *again*, though in a much different way than Rebecca's had. Rebecca's death highlighted the tragedy of losing someone you loved, while Rick's death seemed to
highlight the tragedy of losing yourself and being cut off
from those you love, and who love you. On paper, to put
together a life without Rick shouldn't have been that hard
for me—he was the husband of a close friend of Jennifer's
who we saw a couple times a year—but I found myself
thinking of him, thinking of our weekend, and wishing that
we could have had a chance to say good-bye. It seemed to
be one of the lousy aspects of death, at least some deaths,
that you never really had a chance to say good-bye to the
person who's leaving. One day they just leave, and that is
that.

And this made me think that you not only have to live
each day as if it's *your* last, you also have to live it as if it
is potentially your loved one's last. This means that you
shouldn't put work ahead of the people closest to you, or
put watching the NBA play-offs ahead of the people closest
to you, because if they die while you're watching the
Knicks' offense come to a screeching halt against the Pac-
ers, you wouldn't feel right. You'd think to yourself, "I
didn't make the best choice." You might even think this
about someone who you knew casually. Like a neighbor.
Like the guy at the butcher shop who always asks how the
"mind reading business" is going. Because butchers and
neighbors can die, too. They can die suddenly. Who knows?
Butchers might even be more prone to this because of all
the red meat they eat. So then you have to ask yourself,
"Am I spending my remaining time with my butcher in the

right way? Are our good-byes as meaningful as they could be? Do I truly appreciate the significance of our lives crossing at this point in time?"

Around the same time Rick died, my mother began making plans for Rebecca's unveiling, a Jewish ceremony in which a headstone is placed on the grave approximately a year after the death. And when I say "making plans," I should qualify this by adding that there aren't really a lot of plans to make. An unveiling is much different from a wedding or a bar mitzvah. It is much simpler. There is no band or disc jockey. No fancy dessert tables. No photographer. No personalized napkins with the dead person's name and the date of their death. I wasn't even sure if there'd be flowers involved, but if there were, I assumed they'd be on a much smaller scale. Not a job for a big-time florist. Maybe just some yellow roses like there were at the funeral, something to bring the year full circle.

At the unveiling there'd just be a headstone and a rabbi and some of the people who were there for the funeral. Her friends from New York wouldn't be flying in for this. We would have to make do without their humorous and touching stories. We, the family and locals, would have to come up with some of our own. Actually, I didn't know what we'd have to do. I had never been to an unveiling before. The only funeral I had been to other than Rebecca's was my grandmother's, and I can't remember if she even had an unveiling ceremony. I'm pretty sure my father just decided to have someone at the cemetery put a headstone on her grave and leave it at that. She was eighty-nine when she died.

I hated the sound of the word *headstone*.

And I suppose the purpose of the unveiling was to bring the year full circle, to conclude the first year of mourning and help us make the transition from Rebecca Being Taken from Us to Rebecca Just Not Being Here Anymore. It was a transition I could feel myself making, and I sensed that my mother was making it as well, even though it seemed to be a little slower going for her. Still, she didn't talk about Rebecca quite as much, and I got the feeling that she was starting to feel more a part of life again, as compared to being on the perimeter of life, as she had felt for so many months after Rebecca's death.

"I just hope the unveiling won't be like another funeral," my mother said, and that captured my sentiment exactly.

One notable difference for me between the funeral and the unveiling was that I took care of all the arrangements for the funeral while my mother took care of all the arrangements for the unveiling. She was now in a position where she could "handle it," as she said, and I guess I was in a position where I didn't want to handle it, where I didn't want to immerse myself in the details of cemeteries and plots and headstones and headstone salesmen. Because I assumed there were countless headstones from which to choose, and that they were all different prices, and that there was some guy, dressed in a suit and tie, helping you make the choice that was "right for you." And I didn't want to have anything to do with him or his store or the brochures he might give me to take home.

I preferred to deal with Rebecca's death in my imagination.

I had two dreams about Rebecca after talking with my mother about the unveiling. In the first dream, I was standing naked on a cliff and below me I could see my mother looking for Rebecca in the woods, looking for her as if she were lost, hurrying through the leafless trees, calling out her name, "Rebecca, Rebecca, Rebecca," while I stood on the cliff, naked, not knowing how to tell her she was gone. In the second dream, Rebecca was a potter who made the most beautiful pottery, and that was really all I could remember about that dream, that she made orange, red, and purple bowls and vases that practically glowed from how bright they were. They were not like any bowls or vases I had ever seen.

Mother's Day was coming up, and I really didn't know what to get my mother. More importantly, I didn't know how that day would be for her, didn't know what Mother's Day was like for women who have lost children. I assumed it would be a difficult day, just as Rebecca's birthday had been a difficult day, and I could see how if I were a mother in that situation I might feel a need to have *two* Mother's Days, one for my children who were living, and one for my child who wasn't. Because the experience of being a mother to a living child was so much different from being a mother to a child who had died, and it really deserved to have its own day.

In previous years, I had fallen into the habit of buying my mother Patagonia clothing for Mother's Day—I knew she liked it, but couldn't manage to spend so much money on herself—but on the way to the camping store, I passed a ceramics shop I had never seen before, a place where you could glaze your own pottery. It made me think of the pottery in my dream and what it would be like to try and create something for my mother that was similar to what Rebecca had created. Surely, it would be a more meaningful gift than a Patagonia windbreaker, and I wanted to give my mother something that would be meaningful. I wanted her gift to be something that she could hold on to forever, something that might make her think of Rebecca, something that might make her feel less alone.

The process of glazing the bowl reminded me of when I was a boy and would work so diligently in art classes, so that I'd have something nice to bring home to my mother. I knew she had liked my paintings and drawings, and I had liked being able to give her something. There was even one painting of a bird I made that she kept until I was in high school, until our house was hit by a tornado. And I can remember her looking for that painting in the backyard after the tornado, thinking that by chance she might be able to find it there. Many of our possessions were strewn across our front and backyards, including our '69 Chevy—but my bird painting wasn't one of them.

While I enjoyed the glazing process, I was a little disappointed in the final product. The bowl didn't come out as bright as I wanted, as bright as the bowls that Rebecca had made in my dream. Nevertheless, Jennifer assured me that the bowl was beautiful, and she insisted that I tell my mother about the dream, but that wasn't something I felt like doing, at least not then, at least not on that Mother's Day. I preferred to just give her the bowl and have her enjoy it as a bowl, as something I'd made for her. I assumed it would just be too weird for her to think that it was a bowl that Rebecca and I had made *together* for her, even though that was kind of how it felt.

"I'm so lucky to have you as a son," she said as she unwrapped the bowl and held it to the light. "I can't tell you how lucky I am."

"I'm lucky to have you as a mother," I said, and I did feel lucky, lucky in a way that I'm sure I never used to feel with any of my family when I was growing up.

28

SPEND TIME APART

(and Together)

YOU CAN'T EXPECT to want to spend all your time with
your partner or for your partner to want to spend all their
time with you. A relationship like that wouldn't feel satisfying for very long. After a couple of weeks, it would
probably feel like the trunk of a Toyota, back when Toyota
only made the Corolla and it was even smaller than it is
now. For the record, I once snuck into a drive-in theater
in the trunk of a '74 Corolla, and while it was claustrophobic, it didn't feel nearly as claustrophobic as when I
was in a relationship where I felt I had to apologize for
wanting time to myself.

A problem, or challenge, in most relationships is that
no two people have exactly the same appetites for solitude.
Some people's appetites are very large. Some people have
practically no appetite at all. Then there are those people,
like me, who can waver between both extremes, who can
feel as independent as a cougar (I've already told you about
cougars) one day and as clingy as an infant the next. If you
happen to be in a relationship with a cougar-infant hybrid,

it is important that you put your foot down and let your partner know that if kept up, the flip-flopping back and forth without any transition in between will drive you crazy.

Because the transition between separateness and togetherness plays such a crucial role in relationships; it can be the difference between a relationship that feels as unsettling as a roller-coaster ride and one that feels as reassuring as a drive in a well-made touring car. To continue the automotive analogy just one step further, just as a car wouldn't work well with a transmission that had only first and fifth gears, a relationship doesn't work well when a couple only knows how to completely immerse themselves in each other or completely ignore each other.

Needless to say, this arrangement doesn't work well for the children of these couples either.

Also, if you happen to be a flip-flopper, or a cougar-infant hybrid yourself, you must take some responsibility and try to modify your style of relating. You can't expect that your partner will adjust to you, because if you wait for this long enough, you will run the risk of not having a partner, or not having the same partner, which is a risk that my father took and ended up regretting. And if your hope for a better love lies in finding a partner who will adjust more to you than the one you have now, you might want to give my father a call and hear what he has to say about this game plan. It's likely he will tell you the story about how he and my mother met in Israel. It's likely he will say that "Mom" is different from any woman he has ever met. It's likely he will confess that he'd take her back in a heartbeat if she gave him the chance.

Just as there are people who are scared of togetherness there are also people who are scared to be alone. They associate being alone with feeling lonely, unwanted, and neglected—probably because at some point in their lives they *were* alone and *did* feel lonely, unwanted, and neglected. Needless to say, it is always terrible to feel lonely, unwanted, and neglected, but it is a particularly terrible experience for children. It is so terrible that it can stick with them for the rest of their lives. They can be so terrified of feeling this way again that they will do anything to avoid it, anything from working inhumane hours so they don't have to come home to an empty apartment to staying in a relationship with someone who doesn't treat them well.

And the cruel irony of being in a relationship with someone who doesn't treat you well is that it makes you feel even more lonely, unwanted, and neglected than if you were without someone.

One important thing to remember if you're afraid of being alone is that just because this experience made you feel lonely, unwanted, and neglected as a child doesn't mean that it will necessarily make you feel this way as an adult, particularly if you remind yourself that you don't *have* to feel this way, or don't have to keep feeling this way for too long. It might be that you'll just need to touch base with this feeling at first when you're alone, and then you can move on to something that's less overwhelming, something that might even eventually lead in the direction of self-love.

Does self-love sound like a hokey concept to you? I ask

this because it used to sound like a hokey concept to me, like something that was invented and marketed by the New Age community for workshop purposes; and yet I have come to believe that self-love has utility and validity for all of us, not just for people in California. But the self-love I'm referring to is probably more along the lines of "self-acceptance" than "total bliss," because I must confess that I don't know much about total bliss. I just haven't had a great deal of experience with it. All of my friendships and relationships have been imperfect. They've had ups and downs. They've had their disappointments. And my relationship with myself has been pretty much the same way.

The solitary activities that are most comforting and nurturing to us—and that *do* cultivate something within the realm of self-love—seem to be the ones involving some aspect of creativity or learning. I used to have a wise tennis coach, Art Gaines, who told me that I should approach each match as an opportunity to learn rather than as opportunity to perform, and I have found that it is useful to take a similar approach to other life situations, including those involving loneliness. Because when you can experience loneliness as meaningful, as having something to teach you, it stops feeling like a curse or punishment. Instead, it begins to feel like a third-set tiebreaker that could go either way.

One solitary activity that many people find extremely meaningful is to be out in nature. I know when I'm feeling down or worried about something it always helps me to take a run through the woods or go sit at my favorite spot along the Huron River. And I often thought that psychiatric facilities would have much better treatment success if they were situated at the foot of a mountain or along the ocean. I don't know if you've ever happened to see the inside (or outside) of a psychiatric hospital, but they often don't look like the best places for promoting healing.

For those city dwellers who have absolutely no interest in putting on a pair of hiking boots and dealing with bugs and other hikers and lack of bathroom access, there exists another fine alternative: the café. Cafés are great for those times when you want to be away from your partner, or away from your apartment, and aren't feeling up to or interested in being alone. I think one of the reasons cafés have become so popular—and they've become *really* popular in Ann Arbor—is that they offer a way to be alone without having to be alone. You can sit with a book or a laptop computer and be reminded that your fellow human beings are never too far away, and that what they're wrestling with is probably similar to what you're wrestling with. You can also choose from countless pastries and coffee drinks.

However, when you're sharing your life with someone you must concern yourself not only with your own relationship with solitude and loneliness but also with theirs. You can't just go off and climb a mountain whenever you feel like it, because if you do, you'll make your partner feel as if they don't matter, which is about the worst possible thing you can do in a relationship.

As a couple you have an obligation to do whatever you can to help each other not to feel this way. You can't just take the position that "I'm going to do whatever I need to do and you're just going to have to deal with it." That's not a relationship. That's a person using a relationship. In a real relationship, a couple needs to do all they can to help each other feel secure, even if it involves compromise, even if it involves giving up a weekend opportunity to kill fish or deer. And the reason security is such a wise investment in a relationship is because the more secure your partner is, the more freedom you will have, and the more freedom you both will have to be yourselves.

Then everything gets more complicated when you become parents, because you find that you not only want time away from your partner, but you also want time away from your children; and yet you're not given any more time. Your days are the same length they always were. They're the same length as the days of bachelors. They're the same length as the days of retired people. The gods of time don't take into account that you have to wake up in the middle of the night or do significantly more laundry or take walks that you don't feel like taking just so your child will be lulled to sleep or that at times no one seems to care that you're feeling so pressed for time.

You are probably surprised at how deeply you begin to care about how your time is divided up. You care so deeply that you want to cry, not just because you want time to yourself and can't get it, but because you want more time with your child and more time alone with your partner and more time for everyone to be together, not to mention some time to accomplish a few things professionally, and the math just doesn't seem to work. You feel like a kid who sucks at math, who sucks at math no matter how hard he tries, no matter how hard he wants to be good at it.

Then you discover a way to cheat. It usually doesn't happen until after you've been a parent for a while, when it dawns on you that you have to neglect something, and that it's ultimately your choice what to neglect. You can neglect something important like your marriage, or you can neglect something a little less important like the dust in your house. You can look dust in the eye and say, "Dust, I don't care about you right now." You can even choose to make love instead of dusting. Does that sound crazy? Does that sound like something so crazy that only a man could suggest it? Well, I have news for you: If you don't have the courage to neglect dust and all the things like dust then you will end up neglecting yourself. I guarantee you that's what'll happen, because first you'll give yourself to all the little things that demand something from you, and then when it comes time to take time for yourself, you won't be there.

But even cheating involves a choice and you want to make sure that you don't cheat yourself out of a good memory, that you don't cut so many corners that you're just left with a little blob of a life. The tricky part is that you never know ahead of time what's going to feel meaningful and what's going to feel, for lack of a better word, like a *waste* of time. And it isn't realistic to think that everything about parenthood will feel meaningful, that if you're a man you'll need to be on board for all of your partner's OB appointments, even though your birthing books might suggest that's what the *sensitive* man should do. Because the truth is that most obstetricians and midwives will treat you as if they wish you weren't around. They'll say "hello" and "good-bye" and little else in between. The unspoken message they'll give you is: Go home and paint the nursery if you really want to make yourself useful.

While I missed most of Jennifer's OB appointments for her first two pregnancies, I wanted to be there when she had her amniocentesis, a procedure that we elected not to have with Nikki and Alex, both because Jennifer was a little younger (and the risk of Down syndrome a little lower) and because we didn't have the well-being of two other children to consider at the time. The amniocentesis also took place in the hospital, as compared to her OB's office, which made it seem more serious, probably because it was more serious. The risk of Jennifer having a miscarriage as a result of the procedure was far greater than the risk of having a child with Down syndrome, and yet we both agreed that we didn't want to take a risk with the latter, that it wasn't something we could deal with under the circumstances. For those couples who can deal with a Down syndrome child, or would choose to deal with this challenge rather than have an abortion, there really is no reason to have an amniocentesis. The unpretty truth is that an amniocentesis is mainly for those couples who are prepared to have an abortion.

Another reason I wanted to be with Jennifer for the procedure was that the next morning she was flying to New York to be with Madeline and it was our only chance to spend some time together. In a perfect world, we could have spent some time together in a place other than the University of Michigan Medical Center, but as unsettling as hospitals can be, they can be even more unsettling when you're alone, and I wouldn't have wanted Jennifer to be there by herself, alone to ponder the possibilities of illnesses and accidents and birth complications. It made me think there should be a rule in hospitals, posted on the front door with the other rules about not smoking and wearing a shirt and shoes: YOU CAN'T ENTER HERE UNLESS YOU'RE ACCOMPANIED BY SOMEONE YOU LOVE.

The doctor who performed the amniocentesis seemed very confident in himself, confident to the point of smugness, but it really didn't bother me, since I didn't want an unconfident person sticking a long needle into Jennifer's abdomen anyway. It seemed much better all around that the people who felt the need to question themselves become psychologists or writers rather than medical doctors who are required to use sharp and precise instruments.

I held Jennifer's hand and looked into her eyes throughout the procedure. I didn't want to look at the long needle.

"Soon we'll know for sure if our child's a girl or a boy," Jennifer said the next day as we were driving to the airport, and I happened to be thinking less about the sex of our child and more about her having safe flights to and from New York. And my definition of a safe flight was one where she came back alive, since there didn't seem to be a lot of middle ground, a lot of degrees of safety, when it came to air travel. You either had a safe flight or you had a very unsafe flight. There weren't the equivalent of fender benders once you got that high off the ground. And it suddenly dawned on me that Jennifer and I, since becoming parents, had never flown together, never spent a night together away from our children.

"I'll miss you," Jennifer said as we were about to say good-bye in front of the terminal, and I let her know that I would miss her, too, because I knew I would, knew I would feel temporarily incomplete and out of sorts as I always did when we were first separated. But for some reason, it was easier to think about the unlikely and fantastic possibility of a plane crash than it was to think about this simple incompleteness, this simple longing for us to be together again.

We hugged and I watched her disappear into the terminal, pulling her carry-on suitcase behind her, and afterward, when she was gone, I stood for a second beside our car and just looked up at the sky.

29

APPRECIATE

Where You Came From

WE MIGHT THINK we come from Ohio or New York or California, but once we take a second to consider this, many of us realize we come from places much farther away. This was what happened to me when I watched and listened to the videotape of my mother's Shoah interview: I realized that I came not only from Cincinnati, but also from Warsaw and Siberia and Kraków, places that were much darker at the time my mother was there than Cincinnati was for me. In Cincinnati, there were no bombings, not during the day, and not during the night. There were just Reds and Bengals games, along with UC Bearcats games, which were big in the late '60s when Greg Cook was their quarterback. None of that was a part of my mother's childhood. School wasn't even a part of her childhood after the war broke out.

Her childhood centered on only one thing: survival.

My mother's interview, her life story, provided me with details that helped me to better understand myself and some of the choices I've made in my life, choices rooted in an overwhelming need for self-reliance, a distrust of dependency, a fear of the unknown. Yes, I must confess, that for many years I was afraid of the unknown, and probably still am to a lesser extent. I thought the unknown was dangerous and that I needed to do all that I could to protect myself against it, to control its destructive capabilities. I was a member of the Cover Your Bases Tribe, which is closely related to the Prepare for a Rainy Day Tribe, which in turn is also related to the Don't Count Your Chickens Before They Hatch Tribe.

In short, I lived my life fearing that all of my chickens would be born dead.

I realize that not everyone has the opportunity to sit in the privacy and safety of their own living room and listen to the story of a parent's life, but there are other ways to learn more about where we come from, providing we have the interest. Most relatives, parents included, will be glad to tell their stories, even if it involves a great deal of pain. Maybe *glad* isn't the best word; maybe *invested* is a better one. Because their stories will never be known if they don't tell them, and most of us want to be known before we die. We don't want to die as an unknown person. There is an inherent tragedy to unknownness, a tragedy that probably didn't occur as frequently when we were all a part of a group, comprised of our families and extended families, who had lived in the same spot for countless generations.

I also don't mean to imply that just because a parent might be interested in telling his story, getting him to actually tell it or getting yourself to actually listen to it is an easy task. In some respects, it is much easier to leave the past alone and just make the best of the visits and dinners and rounds of golf that you have left with them. That is probably the approach that most people take, the Easier Life Approach. It is hard to blame anyone for choosing this option, and yet at some point it occurs to many of us that an easier life isn't necessarily a more meaningful life. The problem with an Easier Life—and the problem that many people have with retirement—is that it doesn't really demand anything of us, and as a result, we can feel unneeded, not just by those in our immediate lives, but by the universe. From what I understand, that is one of the challenges of getting older: figuring out how we're needed, how we can keep making the world a better place, even if it's just through touching the lives of our children and grandchildren.

What is challenging about listening to a parent's life story is that it forces us to look at her not just as a parent, as someone who did or didn't give us what we needed, but as a person, as someone who had their own adversity and their own losses, as well as their own joys and passions. It forces us to feel a level of compassion that we might never have felt for her before, and often if we can feel more compassion for what she has gone through, we might also feel more compassion for what *we've* gone through. Our compassion could then keep growing. It could extend to people who've had great injustices done to them, to our enemies, to people whom we no longer even view as people.

As for my mother's life story, as for the videotape of her Shoah interview, I'd like to go back and say that I really *didn't* feel safe while I was sitting in my living room with

Jennifer and watching it. I know I said "in the privacy and safety" of my living room, but that's not really how I felt. Maybe I hoped that I would feel safe, that I'd find what she had to say interesting and enlightening, but nothing more, nothing that would make me feel like a seven-year-old child in Warsaw.

That was how old my mother was when the war broke out, when the bombs began falling. One bomb hit her apartment building and she had to jump from a second-floor window, because the fire blocked the exits. She was afraid to jump, so her mother pushed her. She pushed her the way I would have had to push Nikki. She pushed her the way you would have to push your child. Then one bomb killed a neighbor who was standing only thirty feet away. A piece of shrapnel went right into his head. My mother had trouble sleeping after that. She was afraid that if she went to sleep she would die the way her neighbor had.

I feel obliged to tell you right now that my mother, her sister, and their mother were the only survivors in their family. She came from a large extended family—my grandmother had twelve brothers and sisters who all had families of their own—but none of her aunts, uncles, or cousins survived. I know a better storyteller might choose to keep you, the reader, in suspense, might choose to reveal this information in a chronological sequence—but I don't feel like doing that. I feel like telling you right up front that they didn't survive, that my mother and her mother and sister did everything they could to locate them after the war, but they came up with nothing. And eventually they gave up trying.

It wasn't just the bombs that made me feel unsafe. It was also the blood and the zeppelins and the tanks and the soldiers. My mother had never seen zeppelins before. They looked like monsters to her. The Germans looked like monsters to my grandfather, and he decided to try and sneak his family across the Russian border. That was when my mother woke up next to a man who had frozen to death. Babies were freezing to death all around her, too. They were either freezing to death or suffocating from the smoke of the fires that people made to keep warm. The babies just couldn't tolerate the smoke. And the mothers couldn't tolerate the indifference of the Russian soldiers, who wouldn't let them cross the border into Russia, and so each morning they brought the soldiers the dead babies. Whenever a baby died, they would bring the corpse to the Russian soldiers and lay it at their feet.

It didn't feel any safer to me that they'd then managed to sneak into Russia. That was because the Russian soldiers came one night and made them board a train to Siberia. The train didn't have toilets, heat, or windows. There were just thin slats toward the top of the boxcar, and my grandfather would lift my mother up periodically, so she could see the light, so she could see the world outside. It took them about three weeks to reach Siberia. That was where my mother spent her tenth birthday: in a Siberian work camp. My grandmother asked her if there was no war, and if she could have any present that she wanted, what would it be? And my mother answered, "A loaf of bread."

My mother and her family nearly died of starvation after they were released from the Siberian work camp, and there is nothing that can make you feel as unsafe as hearing about someone you love nearly starving to death. My grandfather actually did die of dysentery while they were in Russia. He died while my mother and her sister were in a Russian orphanage. The orphanage consisted of one large room where all the children slept on the floor. They were each given one bowl of soup per day.

Once the war ended, my mother and her sister went to live in a *better* orphanage in Kraków. There was a school and a student government in the new orphanage, and my mother was elected president. She was sixteen by then, and before her childhood was over, before she would leave Poland and go to Israel where she'd eventually meet my father and where Ezra would eventually be born, she'd have spent eight years of her life in orphanages. She would adjust to orphanage life, would even have some "great moments" in them, as she put it, moments where she felt incredibly alive, where she felt an incredible spirit to keep on living; and yet she was keenly aware of the differences between an orphanage and a home. She would sometimes leave the orphanage in the evening and walk through the streets of Kraków and see the lights in the houses and think, "So many houses, so many families, and none of them are mine."

MY FATHER came for a visit a couple of weeks later, and I thought how much he'd appreciate watching the video of my mother's life story, and yet I knew that wasn't something she'd want him to do. She didn't want anyone to see the video except Jennifer and me, at least not anyone who was a part of her life. The people who came to the Holocaust museums in Washington, D.C., and in Tel Aviv could listen to her experiences, and she felt good about that, and I felt good about it, too. As an adult, I was proud to have a mother who had survived so much, which hadn't necessarily been the case when I was younger, when I was drawn to the domestic calmness of my friends' mothers who were always on hand to make chocolate chip squares or serve up cups of Hawaiian Punch.

The reason a part of me wanted to watch my mother's Shoah interview with my father was because I wondered what it would be like to experience the unsafety with him as an ally, instead of as the person who for much of my life was the cause of my feeling unsafe. And I think it was wondering about this—about the possibility that he could be a source of safety—that made me come up with the idea of going with him to see the Holocaust Memorial Center museum in West Bloomfield, Michigan. My hope was that we could go together and I could feel better than if I went alone. It was a radical hope, or it *felt* like a radical hope, and it wasn't until the last day of his visit that I got up the nerve to actually ask him.

"The kids are probably a little too young for that, don't you think?" my father said in response.

"I was thinking that just the two of us would go together."

"Just the two of us?" he replied eagerly. "That'd be great. That'd *really* be great."

My father is probably the only person who heads to the

Holocaust Memorial Center thinking "This is really going to be great." I would assume that most people head there feeling some form of dread, which was how I headed there feeling, even with my father sitting in the passenger seat beside me. It was the same dread I usually experienced when I sat down to see a film that I expected to be violent; and this dread was at its worst if I knew ahead of time that the violent scenes included some form of torture, especially if the torture took place within the confines of a prison.

And I expected that the Holocaust Memorial Center museum would capture all three of these dread-producing elements for me—that there would be violence, that the violence would include torture, and that the torture would take place within the confines of a prison. What intensified the dread even more than any film possibly could was the realization that it was not a film. It was a piece of history, a piece that included my mother's aunts, uncles, and cousins—as well as the Polish refugees she lived with in the field outside the Russian border. Because what happened shortly after my mother and her family snuck across the Russian border was that all of the refugees in that same field were rounded up by German soldiers and sent by train to concentration camps where they were put to death.

Of course, what my father thought would be really great wasn't the museum itself, but the opportunity for us to spend some time alone together. Ever since my parents divorced my father has been unconditionally receptive to and unconditionally accepting of me, which is something that I try not to take for granted, since I know that fathers aren't always this way. Some fathers never manage to turn the corners of receptivity and acceptance, and if you have a father who is like this, it's imperative that you come to appreciate that it's his problem and not yours; or rather that the problem you have is one of having an unreceptive and unaccepting father instead of being a person who is undeserving of receptivity and acceptance.

I mentioned that we drove to the Holocaust Memorial Center with my father sitting beside me in the passenger seat, and that is because ever since I turned sixteen I promised myself that I would never be in a car with him while he was driving, that I would afford myself the luxury of never having to revisit the powerlessness and terror that I sometimes felt when he was behind the wheel—like on Ezra's sixteenth birthday, like on the last vacation we took as a family to Schenectedy, New York. And it was a promise I never broke, which is a good thing about the promises we make to ourselves as adults.

"Well, here goes nothing," my father said as we pulled into the parking lot and got out of the car, and I realized that one of the advantages of going to a place like the Holocaust Memorial Center with my father, as compared to going there with my mother, was that I didn't have to worry that he would get *too* upset. Emotionally speaking, he was a well-fortified person, which usually felt like a disadvantage when it came to having a relationship with him, but right then, I wouldn't have wanted him to be any other way. He was perfect for me, my well-fortified father heading with me into a seemingly unfortified place.

The Holocaust Memorial Center museum is all underground. There are no windows. You walk through the front doors, pass a security guard sitting at a table, and immediately start descending a ramp toward the exhibits. It is so much darker inside than outside. That was the first thing that struck me: the darkness. It was different from any other museum I had ever visited. It is a museum designed to make you feel. The Nazi speeches and propaganda seem to get louder as you descend the ramp. There are video clips of Hitler in front of thousands of people. The video clips make him seem alive. They make the German people seem alive. Everyone was alive with hate. You can see it in their eyes. You can hear it in their voices. You can just *feel* it.

My father stopped in front of one exhibit, and for a second I thought he was going to put his fist through the Plexiglas. He suddenly seemed unfortified, and I could feel my fortification weakening, too. It happened for both of us at the same time, in front of a photograph of a Jewish man being paraded through the streets of Berlin with his head shaved and his trousers cut. He was being made a spectacle because he had gone to the police for protection against the Nazi terror squads. He was forced to carry a sign that read: I WILL NEVER AGAIN COMPLAIN TO THE POLICE.

My father and I didn't say anything to each other while we were in the museum. We both stopped and looked at the same exhibits. We left them at the same time, walking side by side to the next one. One of the last exhibits was a sculpture—an actual burning flame behind bars—in memory of those who were killed in the Holocaust. I took out a piece of paper from my wallet and wrote down the names of all these places, making sure to spell them correctly. My father didn't ask me why I was doing this. I didn't know why I was doing this.

I just wrote: Auschwitz/BabiYar/Belzec/Bergen-Belsen/ Breendonck/Buchenwald/Chelmno/Dachau/Drancy/Jasenovac/ Klooga/Lwow-Janowska/Maidanek/Mauthausen/Ponary/Ravens-brueck/Sobibor/Stutthof/Theresienstadt/Transnistra/Treblinka/ Westerbork.

"I'm sorry you have to live in a world where things like this happen," my father said as we headed outside, out into the sunlight that was so bright we both had to cover our eyes. And it was the same thing he used to say to me when I was a boy growing up during the Vietnam War.

We then got into the car and started driving back to Ann Arbor, and my father went on to say that he thought what made people different was how long it took for them to feel badly about what they'd done; and how there were some people—like Hitler—who never felt bad about anything. He said most people weren't that way; he said that, sooner or later, most people managed to feel bad. Then he talked about other things. He couldn't seem to stop himself from talking. He told me how his father died when he was two and how his grandfather helped raise him and teach him about Judaism. He even talked about my mother, making sure to emphasize how what he went through wasn't anything like what she went through. You could tell he still had a great deal of respect for her.

"She always had special feelings for you," he then said, as we were getting close to Ann Arbor. "I remember when you were young she'd look at you and say, 'That boy touches my soul.'"

My father talked a little more about my mother, how a part of what he was attracted to was her strength, her ability to overcome adversity, and then we came into town and he suggested we go out to dinner. He wanted to take me somewhere nice, somewhere I wouldn't go to on my own.

"I could go for a good piece of fish myself," he said. "How does that sound to you?"

"That sounds fine," I said, and it did sound fine, going out to dinner with my father, fine in a way that I probably never could have imagined when I was younger, or probably could only imagine when I was *really* younger, before things started to go bad.

30

LEARN FROM
Your Partner

IT SEEMS the bottom line is that a relationship doesn't
work well unless we feel we have something to learn from
our partner. It doesn't matter how much we help around
the house or how complimentary we are or how perfect the
anniversary gift we choose. It still doesn't work. Not really.
Not in a way that touches our soul. And what's the point
of being in a relationship that doesn't touch our soul, especially when none of us know how long we're going to be
here? It just doesn't seem to make sense. Not spiritual
sense. Not mathematical sense. We only have so many
years for our souls to be touched, which means to use any
of those years for some other purpose would be a waste,
at least from the soul's perspective.

The problem that many of us have in relationships is
that we assume that when our soul isn't being touched it's
our partner's fault for not touching it. We don't see it as
a problem of our own openness, because the truth is no
one can touch our soul if we're not open, if we think we're
right all the time, if we're focused on what our partner

needs to learn from us and not what we need to learn from our partner. I will go back to what Art Gaines, my wise tennis coach, once said about approaching each tennis match as a learning opportunity, because I think it applies to our relationships. I think it applies to every morning and evening we spend with our partner.

And thanks, Mom, for keeping your soul open enough to be touched by me.

Admittedly, it isn't always easy to figure out what we should be learning from our partner. Often what we have to learn can frustrate us, can make us feel like rank beginners. I remember reading once that the Zen masters felt a part of their job was to insult their students toward a higher level of enlightenment, and sometimes it seems that our relationships can't help but insult us toward a higher level of love. This doesn't mean that we should go out of our way to insult our partner, or that our partner should go out of the way to insult us—please don't do this, please don't make the mistake of assuming that you're the Zen Master—it means rather that we should all be humble enough to accept our position as students and take our lessons seriously; this includes psychologists; this includes people who write books like this one.

While it might be true that opposites attract, it is also true that opposites teach. A calm person has something to teach an emotional person, and an emotional person has something to teach a calm person. The same is true of a tidy person and a messy person. They both have something to learn from the other. It's not just that the messy person needs to learn to be neater. The tidy person needs to learn to tolerate messes, to accept that to a certain extent life is messy, that families are messy, that love is messy.

However, if we want our partner to learn from us it is also important that we believe we have something to teach. We have to have the conviction that there is wisdom in us, that there is wisdom in everyone. We can't make the mistake of assuming that there is only wisdom in those who have graduate degrees or six-figure incomes or are men. Yes, as crazy as it sounds, there are people who think that only men have wisdom. Some of the people who think this are men. Some are women. Some are Orthodox Jews. I had a client once say to me that after dating countless women, and sleeping with many of them, he had come to the conclusion that they were all basically "airheads."

And if you're wondering if I threw something large and dense at his head, I didn't. I just suggested that he might want to try dating and sleeping with men instead.

Sometimes we fall into power struggles with our partner about who should be learning and who should be teaching, and these struggles always prove to be profoundly meaningless, given that the most important learning in a relationship is always a collaborative effort. That is what it means to *work* on your relationship: to learn *with* your partner about how the two of you can be happy together. Anything where the two of you aren't learning together isn't work. It's something else.

One thing we can all learn from our partners is how we hurt people in relationships. This is an extremely important thing to learn, assuming, that is, that you don't want to continue hurting people in relationships. And I'd like to believe this is an accurate assumption, that the vast majority of us shudder at the thought of hurting the people we love, even though we can't help ourselves at times, even though there are moments when it seems that we've forgotten everything we ever learned about politeness and sharing and apologizing and forgiving.

If you ever find yourself in such a moment, or in such a period in your life, you might want to ask your partner, "Can you tell me how I hurt you?" I promise you that you'll hear something extremely valuable about yourself—so please listen carefully—and that you'll have a better chance of getting back on track with your partner than if you try to convince them that they *shouldn't* feel hurt. Trust me when I tell you that convincing your partner not to feel hurt is as pointless as convincing a cloud that it shouldn't yield rain. The whole process just makes a person feel even more hurt than before.

A common way that most of us hurt our partners is by forgetting for a second that they're not us, that they're separate people with separate ideas and ways of approaching life. It's good, in my opinion, that we are separate people, because I wouldn't want to be in a relationship with someone who was just like me. It'd drive me crazy having to live with someone who *had* to exercise five or six days a week and woke up at five in the morning to write. I definitely wouldn't want to be in a relationship with another writer, with someone who felt compelled to sneak off and jot down a few "ideas" just as everyone was about to eat their dessert.

It is much better for me to be in a relationship with a

person like Jennifer, who doesn't need adversity in the same way that I need adversity, who can enjoy the present without having to gather up sandbags for the future; because while my mother, and father, did an admirable job of teaching me to survive, it was harder for them to teach me how to live, how to trust that life would take care of me.

I remember the most helpful thing that Jennifer said to me during my Restless Period, which came at a moment when I was in a panic about our finances and Nikki's ear infections and our sensual drought, were these four words: "We will be okay."

Another important thing I learned from Jennifer was to see dependency as something that could be strengthening and not just weakening, as something that could eventually lead to a more graceful sense of independence. She taught me this by depending on me and letting me depend on her. She essentially let me depend on her as much as I wanted. She didn't put me on an independence diet, which is never a good way to teach someone to be dependent, and in turn, independent. This is because when you're on a diet you tend to feel starved, and when you're starved, you never feel like moving too far away from the food. Most of the time you are afraid to even take your eyes off it.

And one great advantage of feeling more comfortable with dependency is that you don't have to go around proving how independent you are, how you're independent of people and chocolate and even breakfast. Yes, there was a time when I felt a need to be independent of breakfast, to stay clear of the waffles and omelets and hash browns that were a part of other people's breakfast experiences. My breakfast was a banana. Every morning a banana. In some strange way, I thought this was a sign of character, that I should only have a banana, that I should have less for breakfast than other people did. It makes absolutely no sense now as I recount it.

But two days before Rebecca's unveiling I woke up with a need to have breakfast with my family, a real breakfast with pancakes and eggs and toast with real butter. Not toast with some low-fat spread that was supposed to taste just like butter. And omelets with real cheese, too. From a cow. Not from soybeans. I just didn't care about cholesterol that morning. I didn't care about the different kinds of fat either. I simply wanted to go out to a restaurant and indulge in breakfast with my family. As a desire, it wasn't all that complicated; it was just different for me. I don't know why I had never wanted to go out to breakfast before. Other people did. Every Sunday morning I saw them as I was taking my run, pushing Nikki and Alex in our twin Baby Jogger. Surprisingly, my family never mentioned anything about going out to breakfast either. I suppose maybe it is true, as my father used to say, that an apple never falls too far from the tree.

Jennifer was up for the idea of going out to breakfast. She thought it'd be a great change of pace. This was another way we were different: her initial reaction to a change of pace was that it could be *great*. My initial reaction was that it could be dangerous. Even breakfast. A dangerous breakfast, if that's possible to imagine. And while I appreciated her openness to going out to breakfast as a family, I didn't appreciate how long it was taking her to get ready. I had an appointment at eleven and was afraid she'd use up all of our "breakfast time" washing and drying her hair. It was the drying part that seemed to take forever, the spraying of different moisturizing mists, the intricate brushwork involved. After about ten minutes, I yelled upstairs for her to hurry up, and if you ever want to have a meaningless experience, try holding a conversation with someone who is blow-drying her hair.

"We're not going to have time to have breakfast," I said, helping Alex and Nikki with their jackets.

"We're going to have plenty of time," she insisted, and yet this was what she always thought, right up until the moment she was late.

At the restaurant it dawned on me that if we were going to have any fun I would have to find a way to lighten up a little, to slow down. Nobody wanted to sit down and have breakfast with someone who looked as if he was late for a train, especially if that person was their father. I know, because that's how my father often looked to me, almost as if he believed that the faster he moved through life the less of a chance there was of something bad happening to him. It was a strange blend of superstition and pessimism that I had felt myself before on occasion; it was probably what I felt most of the time when I was afraid.

But when our waitperson came with our menus I realized that there was nothing about breakfast to fear. There were just pancakes and bottles of Heinz catsup and glasses of juice. There was also a poster above our table of a strawberry the size of a beach ball. This captured the attention of Alex, who seemed intrigued by the possibility of such a wonderfully large berry. He was the perfect fruit art fan. Nikki was more interested in the packets of Sweet'n Low. She remembered her nana mentioning that they weren't good for her, and she wanted to know why a restaurant would put something on the table that wasn't good for people.

Then a waitperson walked by with an order of waffles and her attention quickly shifted from the dangers of Sweet'n Low to the possibility of having whipped cream for breakfast. I normally would have pushed for Nikki and Alex to order something more nutritious, but I really didn't feel like pushing for anything. I just felt like being with them. What difference would it make in the scheme of things if they had the breakfast equivalent of a hot fudge sundae? The main thing was that they were excited, and that we were together on a Friday morning when we were usually apart. I even found myself interested in the waffles and strawberries myself. Their excitement was contagious. I couldn't remember when the last time was that I had ordered waffles in a restaurant.

It felt like Thanksgiving when our food finally arrived and we began eating, only it was better than any Thanksgiving I could remember. Nothing felt missing, and that always seems to be a part of my Thanksgiving experience, that someone or something is missing, even though I'm never quite sure what it is. In this Thanksgiving, our Breakfast Thanksgiving, everyone and everything seemed there, including our third child, whom we now knew was going to be a boy. A healthy boy. He was having waffles with strawberries and whipped cream—thanks to Jennifer—right along with us. There wasn't even the awkwardness, as there sometimes seemed to be at Thanksgiving, about who to thank. We were just eating thankfully and trusting that no one would be offended. We were eating the way I think Rebecca would have wanted us to eat.

My only regret was that we didn't get an earlier start, that I had to leave for an appointment in twenty minutes. Twenty minutes of our togetherness just wasn't enough. I was hungry for more of it. Then something incredibly strange happened: I looked down at my watch and discovered that it was nine-thirty and not ten-thirty. Somehow an hour had managed to get away from my close watch, and this usually didn't happen. I usually kept my hours on a short leash, but for once, one of them had run off and I was so happy for it. I was so happy for me. I was so happy for us. I had an extra hour to live however I wanted. It was a gift, this hour, and I was determined to live it as fully as possible, to keep my heart completely open as I sat with my family eating waffles and strawberries.

31

RELY ON FAMILY,

If at All Possible

I SUPPOSE this is one of the challenges of coming to grips
with one's family: figuring out to what extent we can rely
on them. So often, through a painstaking process, we think
we have them figured out, and then they change. They become more reliable. Or more open. Or softer. And we then
have to rethink everything.

Rebecca's and my stories began in the same family, and
while we both went off in different directions in our adult
lives, I'd like to think that our stories, or her story, ended
within the same family, and that it was a family that had
love in it, in spite of some darker moments in its history,
in spite of its inner factions. Our family, like many others,
seemed to have several families within a family, and I suppose the story I have told you has been about the family
consisting of Rebecca, my mother, and me, as well as the
family consisting only of my mother and Rebecca, as well
as the family consisting of only my mother and me.

Rebecca and I never really became our own family until

she died, and then I found myself relying on her more than I ever had before. I know it might sound strange that a man would start relying on his sister *after* she died, but it really didn't feel strange. It felt more natural than *not* relying on her when she was alive. And if you're wondering what you can rely on a dead person for, I'll just say that you can rely on a dead person for everything that you can't rely on people who are alive for, meaning everything related to the Other Side, to Fate, Destiny, Death, and the Unknown. They can serve as a liaison to everything you can't touch, see, or feel. They can be your guide, your angel.

I believe Rebecca has been all of this to me, and that she has even helped me get this story to you.

And people *do* change. I know there are those who think they don't, but I'm not one of them. I'm more from the Do Change School. It is a school that includes my father and mother, a school that includes my brother, Ezra, as well. Because while he had gone on living in the same subsidized apartment and wearing the same "mentally ill" clothes, there were moments when he seemed calmer, moments where he, too, seemed to have the feeling that "everything will be okay." And I will always be grateful to him for one thing: he took care of himself during the year after Rebecca died. He held it together. He took care of himself at a time when I couldn't take care of him, when I couldn't take care of anyone besides myself, our children, and my mother.

Nobody changed in the year between the funeral and

the unveiling as much as my mother did. She died and was born again, died and was born again so many times. She mentioned on more than one occasion that if it weren't for me and my family she probably wouldn't have been able to go on living, and yet I think she would have no matter what the circumstances. She is a woman who isn't dependent on circumstances to go on living, just as she was a girl who wasn't dependent on circumstances to go on living. She went on living in spite of the circumstances, despite bombs, cold, malaria, and near starvation. She went on living when others didn't. That is her story. That is her sister's story. They are the only ones left from their first life. The others became angels the way Rebecca did.

I failed to mention something that my mother said toward the end of her Shoah interview, and that was that the hardest thing she had to cope with in her entire life was Rebecca's death. It wasn't the Nazi invasion or the Siberian work camp or the orphanages. It was losing Rebecca. That is what she said in her interview, and maybe the reason I failed to mention it was because at the time I couldn't fully understand this, couldn't understand how anything could be harder than what she'd gone through as a girl. But I think I might understand it a little better now, might understand that just when you feel all the terrible things in your life are finally over, how devastating it can be when you realize they're not.

It was my mother's fear that the unveiling would feel like a funeral, and it was my fear as well. I felt nervous as I put on my shoes in the morning, the same black shoes I had worn to the funeral and hadn't worn since. They were my death shoes, and I kept them in a closet separate from the others. In time, I would keep them together with the rest of my shoes and would even wear them on days when I wore a black turtleneck and sweater. That morning, though, they still frightened me. I still associated them with the grave and the mound of dirt that was used to cover up the casket. I could still remember having to clean the dirt off my shoes when I got back from the funeral.

As I was lacing up my shoes, I saw a spider crawling down the wall and my first reaction was to get up and kill it, and if Nikki or Alex had been in the room I probably would have, but since I was alone, I just sat and watched it. I watched it for what felt like the longest time until it disappeared behind the dresser. The doorbell rang and our sitter arrived. It felt strange that our baby-sitter was coming over so that we could go to the unveiling. I always associated her coming over with Saturday night and doing something fun.

We listened to a Bob Marley tape—*Exodus*—as we drove to the cemetery. It was one of Rebecca's tapes, one of a few tapes I brought home with me when I went to New York with my mother to clean out her apartment. That felt like a lifetime ago, when I saw my mother sitting heart-broken on Rebecca's bedroom floor, sorting through her scarves and jewelry. I was reminded of the jar of pennies that I gave to the two girls who were sitting outside of Rebecca's apartment, and I tried to picture what they were doing at that exact moment, if they were eating sugar-coated cereal at their respective breakfast tables, if they were still living in the same neighborhood. I would have liked to think that they still *were* living in the same neighborhood, and that they sometimes came to sit on the steps outside Rebecca's apartment.

I have only one remaining recommendation, which is that you might want to try listening to reggae music the next time you have to drive to a funeral or unveiling. Many of the songs are about hope and faith and love, and you can never have enough hope and faith and love when you're on your way to the cemetery. It's much better than having to listen to some rock and roller blaming his girlfriend for everything that went wrong in his life. It can also be nice to listen to nothing, and after *Exodus* was finished, that's what we did.

We were wrong about the unveiling feeling like the funeral. It didn't feel that way at all. There was the same thoughtful rabbi there, and he said kind of the same thoughtful things, but everything else felt different, felt gentler. There were also fewer people. (My father decided that he would come a week later and visit the cemetery on his own, so my mother could have more privacy.) Those who came from out of town for the funeral and the memorial gathering couldn't make it, and I couldn't help but wonder what their lives had been like in the past year, if they had thought of Rebecca at different times, if they had thought of the memorial gathering where the drums were playing and all her friends were together and there was the feeling for me that something was beginning.

At the unveiling I had the sense that whatever had begun would continue on its course, and while at the time it
would have been hard to put into words what this something was, I now think of it as a sense of connection, a
connection that went beyond what I had come to experience with Jennifer, that went beyond sex and couplehood
and all the things related to sex and couplehood, a connection, as ambitious as it might sound, with *everything*,
with girls standing on steps outside of apartment buildings,
with spiders, with aunts and uncles who were killed before
you were even born.

When the unveiling was over—and it didn't last very
long—I walked my mother to her car and hugged her before
she got in, and as I stood in the cemetery and watched her
and my stepfather drive away, watched their car disappear
around the bend, I thought to myself how much more alive
we all seemed a year later, how Rebecca's death had caused
all of us to sink our teeth deeper into life, to appreciate
life as it was happening, not just after it happened or was
about to happen, but right at the moment that it came down
the pike, right at the moment that it took shape.

At least I could say that this was true for me, and as
thankful as I was for feeling more alive, and as grateful as
I was toward Rebecca for helping me with this, it still
seemed like such a shame that she wasn't around anymore,
that she and my mother couldn't spend weekends together
in New York like they used to, that she and my father
couldn't have a few more chances to try and find some
common ground, that she and our children couldn't get to

know each other; and that I couldn't just pick up the phone and call her whenever I wanted, couldn't take walks into town when she came to visit, couldn't sit down at a café and reach across the table for her hand and say, "I love you, sis."

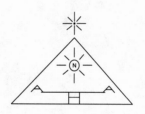